WOMEN IN TRANSITION

WOMEN IN TRANSITION

A course of exercises to help you
get your life in shape

*Based on FACE's 'Women into Work' course developed by Dr Patricia
Putterill, Judith Facey, Barbara Stubbs and Patricia Stone; and other
FACE training materials written by Marcia Parkinson and Michael
Freeney, et al.*

Sara Clay

MERCURY

Copyright © FACE Ltd 1991

17/18 Market Place
Glastonbury
Somerset
BA6 9HL

First published in 1992
by Mercury Books
Gold Arrow Publications Limited,
862 Garratt Lane, London SW17 0NB

Set in Times by TecSet Limited
Printed and bound in Great Britain by
Mackays of Chatham plc, Chatham, Kent

British Library Cataloguing in Publication Data is available

ISBN 1–85251–141–9

Contents

Contents

Contents

Contents

Introduction

This book is based on a course called Women into Work, which was developed by a team of women trainers at FACE (Facility for Access to Creative Enterprise), a national training, research and development company based in Somerset. The course was originally designed for 'women returners', a group typically seen as women who have been at home taking care of the children for a number of years, and who now need a bit of support and encouragement before they can make the transition from home to work.

All of us who became involved in developing and then piloting and editing Women into Work could identify with this group. Our team consisted of a pyschologist plus trainers, writers and editors – all women – who had themselves lived through the sort of career interruptions and life transitions that women regularly face when they have children, defer to their husbands' careers, or cope with other changes in circumstances. The team drew on personal experience, as well as on considerable knowledge of training techniques and resources, to bring together a sequence of exercises that could make a meaningful difference to the way a woman viewed herself, her home environment, and the world she was 'returning' to.

In designing Women into Work, the team didn't try to re-invent the wheel it was largely adapted from widely-used training techniques and exercises. What was significant about it was the effective way in which those elements were combined and used: the sequence of exercises was carefully designed to bring about a process of positive change in each participant's personal development.

By the time we had offered Women into Work two or three times (as part of one of the government-funded training schemes run by FACE), it had become obvious that all sorts of women wanted to do the course who weren't, strictly speaking, eligible for it. We were contacted by women who wanted to move from work to self-employment, from part-time to full-time work, from one sort of work to a different sort. We also heard from women faced with various sorts of personal change, for instance in relationships or family circumstances, as well as women who wanted to make a change. We also drew women dealing with the 'empty nest' syndrome, women who had recently moved to the area and needed help finding their feet and women with a general interest in self-improvement and self-realisation. And, of course, there were any number of eligible women returners who were simply unable to attend a full-time course on the days it was offered. The common thread amongst all these women seemed to be that they were at a point of transition in life, and they were looking for guidance or support in making positive choices for the future.

That is basically why this book came to be written: because so many women were telling us that they needed to do this work. We thought it was important that as wide a range of women as possible should be given the opportunity to access the process of positive change which has made the course so valuable to those women who were able to attend in person.

How to use this book

You are about to embark on a course of exercises, designed to build up specific sets of 'muscles'. These are basically to do with self-confidence, self-knowledge and communication. They are all inter-related, and they all contribute to your ability to take control of your life. Like any exercises, they need to be done in sequence – some serve as a warm-up, others need working up to, many build on strengths and skills developed earlier in the sequence. That would be equally true for a ballet class, a piano lesson, or an aerobics workout.

Introduction

If this *were* a course of aerobic exercises, it's likely that individuals would arrive at the studio with different attitudes and abilities, and with a variety of reasons for being there. Some see an exercise class as a social event, an evening out, an opportunity to meet people. Others might verge on the fanatical about fitness, and dedicate enormous amounts of time and energy to toning every possible muscle. A weightlifter, for instance, would have attitudes and goals which were quite different from those of a fashion model, a figure skater, or a woman getting back in shape after childbirth. All of these people would probably be interested in – and better at – different sets of exercises. But, regardless of their reasons for being there, every one of them would be likely both to enjoy the class and to derive some benefit from participating. They'd all expect to feel good about themselves at the end of the session.

You doubtless have your own reasons for picking up this book, and perhaps a range of hopes or expectations about what it might accomplish for you. Please note that everyone reading it will have a different set of reasons, expectations and needs, and a different background of experience on which to draw. You are quite likely to find, therefore, that some chapters are more relevant to your own circumstances than others, and some exercises more useful to you. However, like the course it's based on, this book is meant to bring about a process of personal development and growth by means of a carefully-constructed *sequence* of exercises. In order to come out at the end with the full benefit, you'll need to do *all* of the exercises, and do them in the right order. Don't skip forward, don't pick and mix – start at the beginning and work through it. Even if you honestly feel that you don't need a particular chapter or exercise, at least have a look at it, think about it a bit, and be clear in your own mind *why* you believe you don't need to do it. That should be enough to 'exercise' the particular set of 'muscles' involved.

You can approach this book as a work-out or a browse-through – you can experience it at whatever depth and in whatever timescale you feel is appropriate. Some people may find it helpful to treat it as a formal course: take notes and keep them in a file, to refer to in later exercises. Others may read it through at one sitting. Both are valid choices. Keep in mind that you're not alone: there will be times when you'll want some support and shared experience, when it will be useful to talk things through with friends, compare notes, and perhaps help each other to reach some conclusions.

It's up to you to decide what you want to get out of this course of 'aerobics'. No problem: the choices will become clear once you've started the 'muscle-building' process, and you'll get plenty of advice and encouragement along the way. This book may significantly change your life; on the other hand, it may simply alter your perspective just a little. Either way, you should feel good about yourself at the end.

1

Identification of skills, abilities and aptitudes – 1

Before you can take control of your future, you have to begin to understand who you are. Knowing yourself, your attitudes, thoughts, ambitions, good points and bad, is essential if you are to negotiate major transitions in your life. And an objective, and fairly painless, way to begin is to look at what you do.

This may seem to be an overly simple approach to self-understanding, but it's a good way to deal with one key factor in our lives: we traditionally undervalue our role and skills. We do it constantly, and unthinkingly. Our response to thanks is 'Oh, it was nothing'; to a compliment, 'This old thing?' And, of course, there is the classic example: when we happen not to be in paid employment – and there may be perfectly valid and honourable reasons why we're not – we're quite likely to describe ourselves as 'just a housewife'. If you ask an unemployed man the same question, he is much more likely to talk (or bluff) about what he is doing, or planning to do.

There are, undoubtedly, countless and complex social, cultural, historical, personal and psychological forces at work behind this regrettable tendency. Other writers have analysed all of them at great length. For the purposes of this exercise, however, we don't need to find something or somebody to blame. We're interested only in results: we want to find out how to turn our automatic responses around, recognise our real experience, learn to state it positively, and put a realistic value on it.

Only when you know what you *really* do, can you decide whether or not you want to continue doing it.

1

Exercise 1: What do you do?

Nobody is 'just a housewife'. Whether or not a woman also has a paid job, at least some of the time she is likely to take on many of the following roles: mother, daughter, wife, sister, nurse, cook, teacher, secretary, handyman, story-teller, taxi driver, entertainer, games mistress, house-keeper, cleaner, hostess, friend, counsellor, peacemaker, policewoman, judge, gardener, organiser, florist, encyclo-paedia, comforter, budgeter, finance controller, sports-woman, hobbyist, committee member, fundraiser, play-group helper, neighbour, PTA member . . . the list goes on *ad infinitum*, and is different for everyone.

Added to all of these are the various roles a woman might be called upon to play in a job or voluntary work. You probably can add several more off the top of your head which are relevant to you. Try writing them all down, without censoring yourself or leaving anything out. The list will be an eye-opener! Keep your list going over a number of days, and add to it as you recognise more of your roles.

Exercise 2: Past positive

So that you can begin to draw some useful conclusions about your own list of roles (beyond 'Goodness what a lot of things I do!'), it will be a good idea to organise them into a format where you can easily look at and analyse them. The exercise we use is called 'Brain Mapping' – a variation on a widely-used technique that makes it easy for one person to brainstorm ideas. It's simple to do, takes relatively little time, and has the added advantage of being fun.

Brain Mapping relies on the process of free association to build up a picture or map of your life, which you can then use to give yourself an overview of what you do and how you feel about it.

First, take a large piece of paper and draw a small circle in the centre of the page. Then write your name in the circle. Branching out from the centre, like spokes on a wheel, you are going to gradually build up a 'map' of your present life. Each branch will represent one of the life roles on your list. (You can refer to the list as needed.)

The example (Fig. 1.1) was mapped out by Judith, one of the group who developed the original training programme, during a session of the pilot course. It covers her own real roles as wife, home financier, gardener, and horsewoman.

To do your own map, start with one of your major roles. Then, using words, pictures, symbols, etc, build up a path for that role. Some people will rely mostly on words, others will use a lot of pictures and symbols – it doesn't matter which you choose. Use symbols and abbreviations that make sense to you. The point is to use anything that can make the process *flow* for you.

Extend each role along its path, including all the activities, sub-roles, feelings and events you associate with it. For example, 'cook' might be extended out to include nutrition, planning, shopping, budgeting/spending, and branch into cake decorating, collecting recipes, competitions, catering, entertaining, and so forth. Depending on how you feel about the various activities, you might add words like 'boring' or 'fun' or 'praise'. Go as far along the line as you can, branching out as appropriate. When you run out of steam, go onto another role and start another line.

It is important to try to work spontaneously and quickly (it is possible to complete the whole exercise in about fifteen to twenty minutes). Try to include *everything* you can think of, in all areas of your life – home, work, family, clubs, church, hobbies. Start with your most important, most time-consuming, or favourite roles, and keep going until you run out of ideas, time or paper. The end result can be as simple or complex as you like. Everyone's map will be different, made up of a wide variety of roles, and with different feelings linked to each role, depending on personal experience.

Once your map is complete, take a few minutes to organise it, using different coloured pens and different symbols (stars, ticks, boxes, circles, and so forth) to indicate each of the following things:

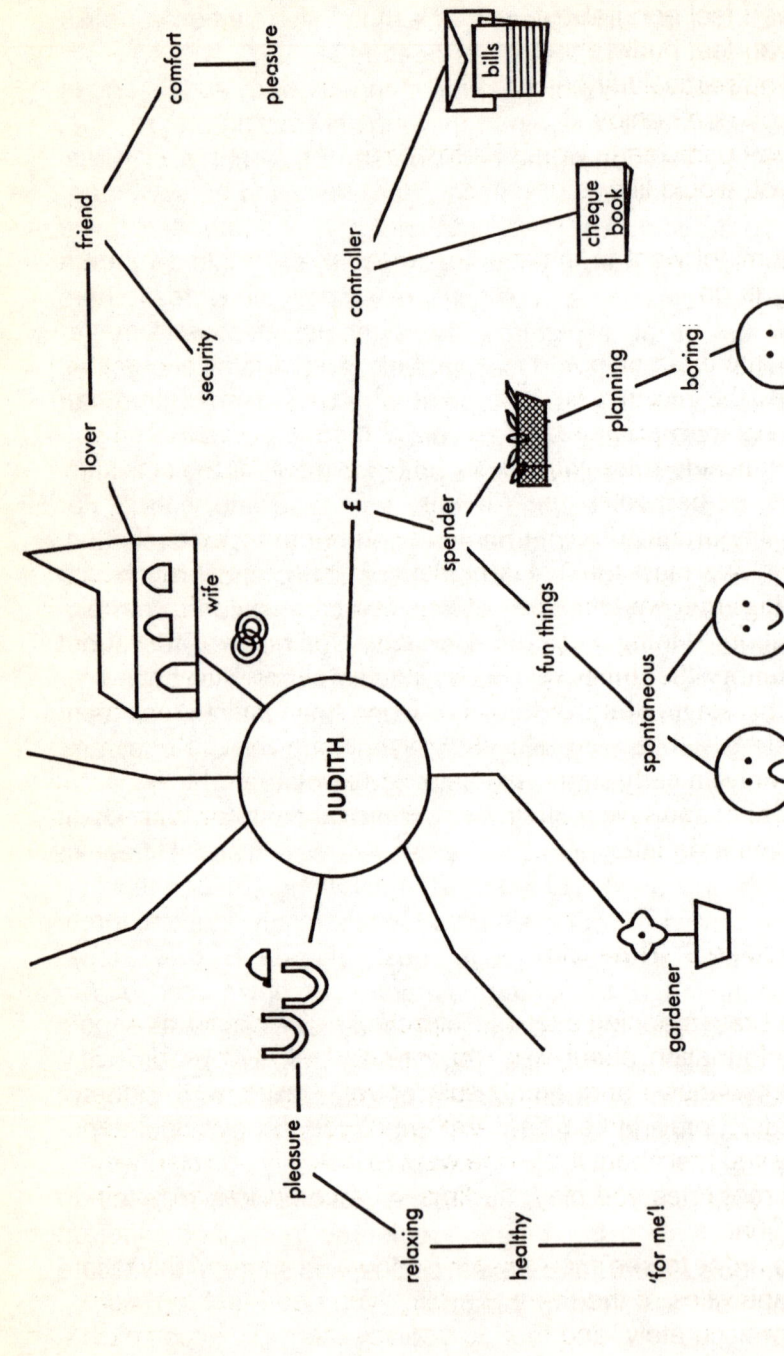

Figure 1.1 Judith's brain map

- that repeat or recur
- you feel good about
- you feel badly about
- you particularly enjoy
- you don't enjoy
- you particularly would like to keep
- you would like to get rid of.

You might want to make a key to the colours and symbols as you go.

So far, the brain mapping exercise has dealt with the present and perhaps the recent past (two to three years). But if you feel it would be appropriate to your own situation, you can extend your map to include roles you played earlier in your life – particularly if there are past roles that you miss.

It is important to recognise *all* the roles in our lives, past and present. We must look back realistically at the past, and accept the things that we feel badly about, as well as the things we feel good about. Doing so can help us move forward into the future and identify the things we do and don't want to change.

At this stage, you may begin to draw some conclusions about your life based on your map. Resist the temptation. Remember, this is only an early step in an ongoing process. Put the map aside for a while, and save it to use as a reference point for some of the work you'll do later.

Exercise 3: Time trial

The brain mapping exercise helped to pull together a range of information about who you are and what you do, in a spontaneous – and highly subjective – fashion. In other words, it provided a first look at what you *think* you do, and how you feel about it. Next we want to identify and clarify the different roles you play, this time in a completely objective fashion.

In order to see more clearly, and value more highly, the complexities of the roles you play, you need first to record them accurately, and then to analyse them. To accomplish

5

this you'll need to keep a diary of how you use time, over a specific period. For this particular exercise, you'll want to record a 'typical' 24-hour day. The objectives are:

- to find out exactly how you use your time;
- to look at what roles you play every day;
- to look at how often you play the same roles;
- to look at how many different roles you play; and
- to provide information which you will find useful later in the process.

[*Note*: This is the sort of exercise some people may find tedious. The thing to remember, as any aerobics instructor would tell you, is – 'NO PAIN, NO GAIN'. Don't resist. Think about how good it is for you, and just get on with it. You'll be glad you did it in the end.]

The best sort of diary to use is one with a line for every hour of the day (Fig. 1.2). If you prefer, you can rule an ordinary notebook in the same way. Divide the day into three vertical columns: in the first column, you'll record each activity and time spent at it; in the second, the *role* you played in that activity; and in the third, any comments you might have.

In order to make sure that you remember to record your activities completely and accurately, keep the diary in an obvious place, where you're sure to be reminded. It is all right to estimate time spent. Ideally, however, you want to build up a fairly precise record, so the best time to make your notes is immediately on finishing each separate activity if you can. However you decide to go about it, don't wait until the next day.

Review

Once your record is complete, think about the roles you've played in the following ways (again, using different coloured pens to code them will make it easier to analyse):

- *Similarities of roles played.* Do a number of your roles involve the same basic skills (such as planning, or

6

Time record sheet

Hour	Time used/activity	Roles played	Comments
0000			
0600			
0700			
0800			
0900			
1000			
1100			
1200			
1300			
1400			
1500			
1600			
1700			
1800			
1900			
2000			
2100			
2200			
2300			

Figure 1.2 An example of a time record sheet

showing sympathy, or paying attention to detail)?

- *Differences in roles played.* In what ways are they different? Are there no similarities at all?
- *Variety of roles played.* How many different roles did you take on in the day? How does that compare with your original list of roles?
- *Repetition of roles.* How often did the same role come up in the day? How much time do you spend at it?
- *Number of roles played within a given time.* Were there times in the day when you took on several different roles in succession within a short period? Is that the exception or the rule?

Exercise 4: Skills analysis

Having just demonstrated that you regularly play a wide variety of roles, you can now begin to look at the skills involved in each of the roles you play. It's important to remember that *no matter how good or bad you are at playing a role, or how much you might like or dislike it, you are using a set of skills to do it.*

If, for example, one of your roles is 'taxi driver' – ferrying the kids back and forth to school, running errands, and so forth – you are using the following skills (and please feel free to add any more you can think of):

TAXI DRIVER

driving skills
knowledge of the Highway Code
knowledge of local roads
estimating distances
planning the best route
organising fuel
organising people for pick-ups
vehicle maintenance
memory
being on time
estimating time
(add any more you can think of)

These are all useful skills. They can be as useful to an employer as they are to your family. And, obviously, any skills involving such things as 'organising', 'planning', 'memory', and 'being on time' are highly desirable in any sort of job, not just one that involves driving.

You could draw out a list of skills for every role you play, ad infinitum. That brings us to the final exercise in this chapter: make another three-column list. In column one, write each of your roles; in column two, list all of the various skills you can think of that are involved in doing each role; in column three, try to think of all the different situations – whether at work or in other contexts – where those skills might be used. Take as much time as you need to give it serious thought.

Keep your skills list for future reference. We'll come back to your diary in Chapter 4.

2

Goal setting

If you don't know where you're going, you'll probably end up somewhere else. This is particularly true for those of us who got lost in the confusions and conflicts between our hopes and ambitions and what we feel may be open to us.

There are undoubtedly numerous dedicated doctors and ballerinas out there who decided at the age of twelve what they wanted to do, and then did it. Those admirable women are neither reading – nor, for that matter, writing – this book. The rest of us are likely to have been diverted into a 'suitable' career by parents and teachers who had our best interests at heart; or perhaps we took a 'career' break to raise children, and then took whatever job we could find merely because the location or hours were convenient; or perhaps we deferred to the needs of our husband's 'more important' career. And there may even be a few of the above-mentioned ballerinas who have come to the end of their dancing careers, and are now faced with the prospect of trying to begin all over again at something entirely different.

What we have in common is that, having encountered our respective diversions, setbacks and blocks along the way, we have now arrived at a point in our lives where we recognise the need to get back on track. We can do this, and then maintain direction, by first learning to set clear goals, and then setting achievable action plans.

Exercise 1: What do you want to do?

By the end of this chapter, you should be able to produce a list of your long-term and short-term personal goals; rank your goals in terms of their importance to you; and then review and reassess those goals. This is a five-step process.

Step 1

Simply *list* your goals. Write them down, as quickly as possible. You should include:

- things you want to achieve, now and in the future
- things you want to do, now and in the future
- things you want to happen, now and in the future.

What you should end up with is a fairly mixed bag of 'wants'. Not all of them will be important, some might seem impractical, many very specific and 'do-able', others quite abstract. The following example will give you an idea of what might end up on a typical goals list.

   I want:

> to put the car in for a service
> to be happy in what I do
> to live on the moor
> to get the shower in the bathroom connected
> to get an interesting job
> to go on holiday abroad next year
> to earn over £10,000 a year
> to go on a world cruise
> to keep chickens
> to go out with friends at least once a month
> to join a folk group as a singer
> to finish knitting my jumper

Now it's your turn. Go for quantity, not quality. List goals quickly, as they come to mind. Don't try to put them in order of priority or timescale. Put down *everything* that comes to mind, no matter how incredible, ridiculous or trivial it might appear. You'll get a chance to sort them out later. *Do not censor yourself!*

Step 2

Sort the list by timescale. Depending on when you want to achieve each of these goals, categorise them as follows:

I want to achieve this goal: within the next month   M
within the next year   Y
sometime in the future   F

For example:
I want:

to put the car in for a service	M
to be happy in what I do	M
to live on the moor	F
to get the shower in the bathroom connected	M
to get an interesting job	Y
to go on holiday abroad next year	Y
to earn over £10,000 a year	F
to go on a world cruise	F
to keep chickens	Y
to go out with friends at least once a month	Y
to join a folk group as a singer	Y
to finish knitting my jumper	M

Step 3

Determine how important you think each of your goals is to you. Mark your goals 'A', 'B', or 'C' ('A' is the most important, 'C' least important). Work quickly, don't agonise – trust your instincts! You want to find out what you really feel, not what you *think* you feel, or what you think you *should* feel. For example:

12

I want:

A	to put the car in for a service	M
A	to be happy in what I do	M
A	to live on the moor	F
B	to get the shower in the bathroom connected	M
B	to get an interesting job	Y
A	to go on holiday abroad next year	Y
B	to earn over £10,000 a year	F
C	to go on a world cruise	F
C	to keep chickens	Y
A	to go out with friends at least once a month	Y
B	to join a folk group as a singer	Y
B	to finish knitting my jumper	M

Step 4

Cross out all the Bs and Cs – you just said they're less important. At this point you may feel compelled to regrade some of your Bs and Cs – that's perfectly OK. On the other hand, please note that crossing out your B and C goals doesn't mean they're not still perfectly acceptable and achievable. They are just less important to you at the moment. Remember, *you* are the one who graded them. We'll regrade 'get an interesting job'. This leaves:

I want:

A	to put the car in for a service	M
A	to be happy in what I do	M
A	to live on the moor	F
A	to get an interesting job	Y
A	to go on holiday abroad next year	Y
A	to go out with friends at least once a month	Y

Step 5

Rank your A goals in order of priority, starting with A1 as most important, A2 next, etc. (You're only allowed one A1,

13

one A2, and so forth.) Again, don't agonise over choices – trust your instincts, and work quickly. Example:

I want:

A6	to put the car in for a service	M
A1	to be happy in what I do	M
A4	to live on the moor	F
A3	to get an interesting job	Y
A2	to go on holiday abroad next year	Y
A5	to go out with friends at least once a month	Y

Exercise 2: Action

When you've finished, write your A1 goal at the top of a new page in your file, and spend a few minutes making a list of everything you might need to achieve that goal. This list will probably be a diverse mixture of things including, for instance, resources needed and actions that have to be taken by yourself and by others. (You have just completed the first step in action planning. We'll come back to that a number of times later, starting in Chapter 3.)

Having worked through Steps 1 to 5, there are a number of conclusions we can draw about this goal setting exercise. Firstly, setting goals gives us direction; and second, putting them in order of priority helps us to achieve what we most want. This process helps us to concentrate our time and energy on achieving our most important goals, rather than wasting them on lesser goals.

It's also important to realise that our goals will change through time, as we achieve them, or as our lives and circumstances change. This process is both natural and inevitable. From time to time, therefore, we need to recategorise our goals in terms of importance and priority, and set new goals. In future, we should aim to do this every six months at least. However, for practice, we are going to do it again shortly, and in later exercises.

Exercise 3: Review

Goal setting is an activity that needs to be done regularly and reviewed frequently. Goals are not carved in tablets of stone. They change as you change. It is important, therefore, to take time to clarify and reassess your goals.

Wait a few days after writing your original list of goals, and then look back over them, working through the following tasks as honestly as you can.

Questionnaire

1. Are there any other goals that you would like to add to the list? If so, add them to your list now.
2. Are there any goals that you would like to take off the list (because, for instance, you've achieved them or changed your mind)? If so, take them off the list now.
3. Are there any things you would like to do, but have not written on your list because you felt they were:
   – too difficult
   – too silly
   – too daunting
   or that you left out for any other reason? If so, add them to your list now.
4. On a separate sheet of paper, draw up a new goals list, making sure to include all your additions and alterations.
5. Now re-order your goals in terms of time. When do you want to have achieved each goal? (M – within one month; Y – within one year; F – at some time further in the future.)
6. Now re-order your goals in terms of their importance to you. Try to ignore, at this stage, how practical the goals may be.
7. Make a separate list of all your A goals in order of priority (A1 first, A2 second, etc).
8. Find somewhere to keep the list so that it's readily available if you need a reminder (for instance, on a notice board by your desk or at the front of your diary).

Now ask yourself the following questions: Has your list of goals changed as a result of the review process? How? Will it be easier to achieve goals if they are written down and analysed in this way? How often do you think you should review your goals? How useful did you find this exercise?

Exercise 4: One last thing to try

This method can also be used very effectively for day-to-day targets. Make a list of things (goals) you'd like to accomplish in the next 24 hours, and prioritise it in the same way. Then see what happens.

Points to remember

- Goals give us direction.
- Goals can be changed and adapted to suit us.
- As we achieve one goal, it is important to set a new one.
- Goals may seem difficult to achieve, but if they are important to us, we should at least have a go at achieving them.

Repeat this process of goal setting and review two or three times over the next few weeks.

3

Action planning – 1

Successful action planning is like most things in life – easy if you know how. Women are used to planning quite complex things. Sorting out transport, timing, equipment and nourishment for the entire family's individual activities on an average weekend, for instance, takes a fairly high level of planning ability. People who do similar things for a two-day business conference are paid extremely well for using precisely the same skills.

Whether in a home or business setting, we've all had to do something along those lines at one time or another – and we've probably done them pretty well. Strangely, however, women often doubt their own abilities and skills. We don't stop to think about it. We just get on with it, without ever realising how much we've actually accomplished.

The fact is, you are probably fairly well organised already – at least when you need to be. You could never get everything done if you weren't. If you don't think of yourself as an 'organised person', the following exercises may help to prove that you are. In any case, they'll certainly help make it a bit easier to get things done. Remember: action planning is simple.

Exercise 1: Simple action planning

At the end of Chapter 2, you prioritised your 'A' goals in order of their importance to you, wrote your A1 goal at the top of a sheet of paper, and started a list of all the things you might need in order to achieve that goal. For this exercise, you might want to continue working on that goal, or you may decide to choose another. You'll want to choose something practical and reasonably straightforward to achieve within one week. In any case, don't get too ambitious at this stage. We are not trying to transform your life in seven days — we are simply testing a technique.

Write the goal you've chosen at the top of a sheet of paper, and then rule six columns, as follows:

GOAL: *(write in your goal)*

What has to be done	Priority A,B,C,D	When by	Who by	Resources needed	Completed

---

Now list separately each task that must be done in connection with your goal, filling in the other columns as you go. Try to keep your planned 'actions' close to you in terms of responsibility. The further away they are, the less likely you are to have any influence on what happens.

For each action:

- decide on a specific timescale;
- work out what resources you will need;
- allocate responsibility for carrying out each action;
- think about what support you will need; and
- keep it realistic.

Note: This exercise is not a sprint. You'll get your best results if you think it through carefully, so take your time.

Once you have thought of every task necessary, prioritising your actions is probably the most critical step. Fortunately, it's a straightforward process. First decide whether each task is Urgent or Not Urgent, then whether each is

Important or Not Important. Tasks which are Urgent and Important are Priority A, Urgent and Not Important are Priority B, Not Urgent but Important are Priority C, Not Urgent and Not Important are Priority D. Do them in that order.

The final column ('completed') will be filled in as each task is accomplished, in the next part of the exercise.

Exercise 2: Action

Having completed the planning exercise, the logical follow-up is to put your plan into action in a *Seven-Day Plan*, as follows:

Step 1

Do it. Fill in the date you complete each action, so that you can compare it with the deadline set in the 'When by' column. Keep simple notes on what happens, both positive and negative.

Step 2

At the end of seven days, analyse your success in carrying out your action plan. Specifically look at:

- one thing that went well
- one thing that went badly
- one thing that was unexpected
- one change that you made.

You'll be building on the information and experience gained in this exercise in later chapters.

4

Time management – 1

Time – and how it is spent – can be a major issue for women who are contemplating or dealing with change in their lives. New goals, such as returning to work, taking on new responsibilities, retraining, starting a business or other changes, can increase the time demands on your already busy days. New goals can also create knock-on effects within the home, and in relationships. We may find ourselves needing to:

- reallocate time;
- delegate certain tasks and work; and
- redistribute our own current time use.

There are two alternative reasons why you are likely to need to look at how you allocate your time.

- Your time may already be fully committed to such things as your home and family, your job, community work, clubs, social obligations, and so forth. If that's the case, you will need to learn to shed roles and reallocate tasks in order to achieve your new goals.

- Alternatively, it may be that your children have left home, or perhaps you've been made redundant, or for some other reason you now have time on your hands, and are looking for the best possible use for it. You already have the time available to achieve your goals, but you may want to clarify them, or to build the confidence to tackle them.

In this chapter, we'll begin the process of learning to manage time by looking at your current time distribution. By the end of the chapter, you should be able to:

- produce a representation of how you currently distribute your time;
- identify which areas of your life you find satisfying; and
- highlight areas of your own time use that need to be expanded, contracted, maintained or shed.

Exercise 1: Time portions

First, we'll look again at how you use your time. Draw a circle about six inches in diameter. Then think about what proportion of your time is used on different activities, and divide up your 'pie' accordingly. Remember, this is not expected to be an exact representation of your real time use, merely an approximation. On the example pie chart below, for instance, you will note that there seems to be more time spent travelling than sleeping!

Figure 4.1 Pie chart to show estimated time use

Time used

When you've finished, turn your chart face down. Draw another circle on another piece of paper, but this time, think about where you get your satisfaction from. *Do not look at the first chart whilst you do the second one.*

Figure 4.2 Pie chart showing satisfaction gained from activities

Satisfaction gained

Now compare the two charts. Use different coloured pens to indicate each of the following:

- anything that appears on the satisfaction chart, but not on the time chart;
- anything that appears on the time chart, but not on the satisfaction chart; and
- any differences in the size of the segments.

For instance, on the example charts such things as riding, travel and holidays are all apparently great sources of enjoyment to this woman, according to her satisfaction chart. But they don't appear on her time chart at all. Nor does spending time with friends, unless she goes shopping with them! Looking at the charts, she might recognise a possible need to allocate more time to gardening, and to try for more 'quality time' with her family, rather than 'house' (which probably means cleaning) and 'cooking'.

Fortunately, in this case, work seems to be this woman's greatest source of satisfaction. She allocates it an even bigger part of the 'satisfaction' pie than she did of the 'time' pie – although it was the largest part of both. And that might indicate that if she wants to make improvements in her time use, she wants to look at how she allocates her time *outside* work.

Now look at your own charts side by side, and think about the following questions:

- What differences did you find between the time chart and the satisfaction chart?
- In light of your new goals, what segments on your charts would need to be expanded, contracted, maintained or shed?
- What difficulties might these changes generate, and how will you deal with them?

Make brief notes, if it helps you to remember. We'll come back to them later.

Exercise 2: Time keeping, revisited

Of course, the charts you've just done are only approximations. The next step will be to produce an accurate, objective picture of your time use to compare them with. To do this, we'll carry on with the diary started in Chapter 1. This time, you'll want to record a 'typical' week (including the weekend), so that you can get a clear idea of any patterns that are established in your life. Your objectives will be:

- to find out exactly how you use your time
- to look at what roles you play every day; how often you play the same roles; and how many different roles you play
- to clarify how your current roles relate to your perceived sources of satisfacton in life
- to provide information which you will find useful in later exercises.

23

If possible, use a diary with one day per page and a line for every hour of the day (or rule an ordinary notebook). Again, you're going to divide each day into three vertical columns: in the first column, record each activity and time spent at it; in the second, the role you played; and in the third, any comments you might have.

This time your comments will be the most important element. Think about the *satisfaction* you derive from the particular activity; how it fits into your list of *goals*; whether it's desirable or possible to *reallocate* that particular activity. If your pie chart (like the example) has monolithic wedges called things like 'work' or 'house', try to break them down into their component roles, so that you'll be able to see which parts of your job, for instance, take up most time, and which are the most satisfying.

In order to make sure that you finish with a complete and accurate record, it will be a good idea to write your diary entries regularly, at the same time and place. Keeping the diary in an obvious place, where you're sure to be re-minded, is also helpful. It's all right to estimate time spent, but for a really precise record, the best time to make your notes is immediately on finishing each separate activity, if that's convenient. In any case, try not to leave it until the next day.

At the end of a week, check through to see whether your record is complete. Don't forget to include at least one weekend. You should have enough reasonably accurate time-keeping to give a balanced picture of your activities. Depending on how good your memory is, you *are* allowed to fill in any blanks at this stage. However, if there are too many holes in the diary to give an honest overview of your time use, carry on with the exercise for a few more days, until you have a complete week.

Exercise 3: Review

Once you have a complete record, you can begin to analyse your diary. As in Chapter 1, think about your time use in terms of:

- similarities of roles played
- differences in roles played
- variety of roles played
- repetition of roles
- number of roles played within a given time.

Use a different coloured pen to mark each different role. Scan down your comments column, noting with different symbols (ticks, stars, crosses, question marks and others) areas of satisfaction, the times when you seem to be fulfilling your goals, which activities you might want to eliminate, expand, reallocate, and so forth.

Ideally, at this point it would be good to create perfectly accurate pie charts of time use and satisfaction based on the timings you've established in your diary, so that you can compare them with the two you sketched last week.

If you are able to feed the figures into a computer and come out with that sort of graphic, by all means do so. Or, if you're a dab hand with a calculator and protractor, and you want to translate time into percentages and then into degrees of a circle, carry on. On the other hand, you might prefer to do a bar chart on graph paper. Use one line per role, and fill in one square per hour. Again, you might want to group similar roles or activities together, and use different colours or symbols to denote satisfaction, goal fulfilment, and any other classifications that make sense to you. For example:

Gardening		++++
Cooking		+++++++++
Shopping		– –
House:	Cleaning	××××
	Decorating	++++
Work:	Writing	★★★★★★★★★★★★
	Admin	××××××××××

Conclusions: Gardening, cooking and decorating are satisfying to this person, cleaning and admin are not, shopping is neutral, writing fulfils goals (and is satisfying), and so forth.

Compare your results with your original pie charts, and note any significant differences between your perception of what you do and what you really do. Reconsider the set of questions we raised earlier:

- What differences did you find between the time charts and the satisfaction charts?
- In light of the goals you've set for yourself, what segments on both your charts would need to be expanded, contracted, maintained or shed?
- What difficulties might these changes generate, and how will you deal with them?

You will find it useful to talk through these questions with a friend. Remember, if you are going to progress, your time may need to be redistributed or reallocated, and tasks may need to be delegated to others or altered to become more manageable.

5

Managing change

'Managing change' has become something of a buzzword in business today. Whole companies do courses on it, from chief executives down to assembly line workers. Consultants specialise in it. In a sense this book is all about managing change on a personal level. (In fact, if it weren't for some of the unhelpful connotations attached to the words 'woman' and 'change' when used in the same sentence, this book might have been titled something like 'Women and Change'.)

In this chapter we'll be dealing with the process of identifying changes needed for personal growth and development in order to achieve aims. When we've finished, you should be able to:

- understand the dynamics of change;
- identify one specific change you want to achieve in the next few weeks;
- experience the transition process of change;
- record the process of change for future use; and
- identify your personal style of coping with transition.

Change – no matter how small a change – is the key to creating a different environment for yourself.

In this chapter we'll be dealing with the process of identifying changes needed for personal growth and development in order to achieve aims. When we've finished, you should be able to:

- understand the dynamics of change;
- identify one specific change you want to achieve in the next few weeks;
- experience the transition process of change;
- record the process of change for future use; and
- identify your personal style of coping with transition.

Change – no matter how small a change – is the key to creating a different environment for yourself.

Exercise 1: All life is about change

All of us experience change, whether it is imposed on us or planned by us, whether it gradually creeps up on us or just seems to fall out of the sky. You might say that changes happen in two ways:

- Some changes *happen* to you. Events can overtake you, and there's nothing you can do about it – whether these events are positive or negative, they're outside your control. They might include such things as redundancy, illness, bereavement, a job offer or a financial windfall.
- Some changes are *planned*. You can deliberately change the circumstances of your life, either because you're not happy with your situation, or because the change will bring rewards or satisfaction that cannot be achieved unless you do something new.

Try to remember that any transition, no matter how unwelcome, offers the chance to grow and develop. Change equals possibility. And, regardless of whether you carefully orchestrated the change or it caught you entirely by surprise, you can identify the process of transition that occurs within it.

Psychologists have analysed how people deal with change on a personal level in terms of a seven-stage model (Fig. 5.1). As we experience the various phases, our self-esteem goes up and down, roller-coaster fashion.

Think about a change you've experienced in the past and see whether it followed this model:

Stage 1: *Immobilisation.* The initial reaction is a down-turn. 'It can't have happened to me.' 'I can't do it.' 'I don't know what to do.'

Stage 2: *Immunisation.* Denying the problem, or minimising its importance allows spirits to rise temporarily. 'It won't affect me very much.' 'Perhaps if I tried I could do it.'

Stage 3: *Depression.* Rock bottom. The black hole. (And we've all been there.) 'I can't do it.' 'It's awful.' 'I can't see any way forward.'

Stage 4: *Acceptance of reality.* Letting go. Realising the worst is over (and then, of course, the worst *is* over). 'It *has* happened to me. I have to begin to plan for the future.' 'It's not exactly the way I planned it, but maybe with some adjustments I could still achieve part of my goal.'

Stage 5: *Testing.* Actively (if tentatively) seeking solutions, and beginning to climb out of the trough. 'That wasn't too bad, but I wonder what would happen if . . .?' 'I can't do *that*, but maybe if . . .'

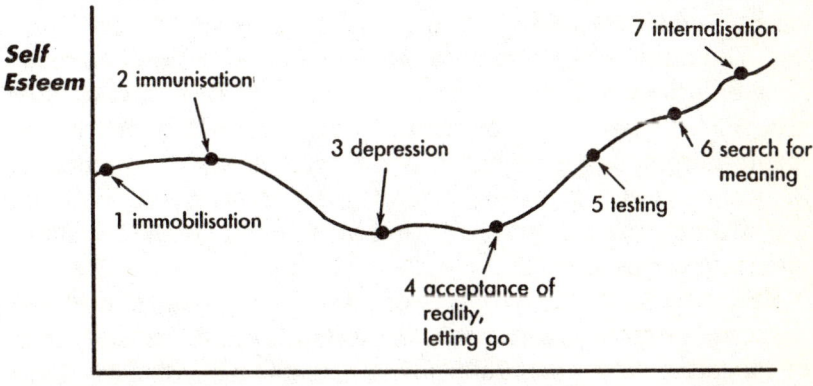

Stage 6: *Search for meaning.* You're definitely upwardly mobile. Everything is part of the plan, a learning experience, therefore all change is potentially valuable. 'What are the wider implications of my actions?' 'I see where this fits in.'

Stage 7: *Internalisation.* Now you're at the top of the charts, with a lot of energy to spare. What has happened has become part of you, has made you a better person. 'I understand.' 'I can play my part.' 'I know my value.' 'It's come right.'

This seven-phase model is a cycle of experiencing a development, gradually coming to terms with its reality, testing out new forms of behaviour and new ideas, understanding yourself, and then incorporating the change into your own life. Your level of self-esteem will change as you go through the seven phases, but you can't expect it to follow a smooth, predictable path.

People rarely move neatly along from Stage 1 through to Stage 7 in precise order. One person might not get past minimisation, another will get stuck in depression, others will quickly get to an active phase, but then fall back to a state of immobilisation. Have you noticed how much soap opera psychology centres on the denial or 'immunisation' stage? ('Poor thing, she hasn't taken it in yet.' 'He is no longer my son.' 'I don't want to know.')

For a transition to be effective, all seven phases probably have to be worked through. Any change – even a planned and desired change – involves letting go, for instance, and that means grieving. You might be delighted to move to a larger house in a better neighbourhood – but once there you may well miss (find yourself 'grieving' for) your old neighbours, or even a particularly convenient shop. However small the required dose, the sooner we allow ourselves to grieve for whatever it was, the sooner we move forward and benefit from new opportunities that the transition opens up for us.

Everyone has different ways of coping with transition. These might range from vigorous furniture polishing, to massive doses of chocolate, to aggressive behaviour, tears or depression. If you understand your coping skills, and then channel that energy into

30

positive action, it can help you make a successful transition through change.

You may have noticed that a good number of our exercises so far have involved making lists. This is a classic coping skill – and highly useful if you want to manage change, rather than letting change manage you.

The corporate woman

So far this introduction to transition has concentrated on you as an individual moving though change. But transition is most effective when it involves the group or organisation in which the 'mover' operates. Remember, the 'mover' is the key agent of change. Without *her*, nothing can be achieved.

Picture yourself as a sort of corporate individual. You might like to refer to the work you did earlier on roles, skills and time use, in order to establish the various 'departments' or 'subsidiaries' of your personal limited company. Your 'company structure' chart might look a bit like your brain map. (And if any company were active in as many different areas as you probably are, it would probably be a huge multi-national conglomerate. You can hardly call yourself 'limited' – *unlimited* is more like it.)

The various people in your life – family, friends, tradesmen, co-workers, etc – will fit into your company structure as clients, colleagues, suppliers or employees. Obviously the same people might fall into a number of different categories at different times, depending on which role or 'department' you're operating. They're your clients when they 'buy' your goods and services; your colleagues when they are working with you to achieve a particular goal; your suppliers when they provide your raw materials, or when your activities depend on their prior work; and they're your employees when you delegate responsibilities to them.

Exercise 2: The managing change checklist

Bearing all that in mind, take a look at another seven-stage model for the management of change. This one is called the

Managing Change Checklist, and is based on work done by the Employment Department's Economic Development office. It is normally used to help take organisations through necessary transitions, as they change their methods of operation in order to survive in a constantly changing business environment.

Many of the checkpoints on this list can be just as useful to the individual who is coping with or, preferably, preparing for changes in personal circumstances. Stretch your imagination a bit, and think about how you would apply it to your own situation. (Our comments/explanations are in the right hand column.)

Stage 1: *Commitment to change*

- Create the vision.

  What do you ultimately want to achieve?

- Spread the word.

  Tell everyone who's likely to be involved or affected. Also, the more people you tell, the stronger your own commitment is likely to be.

- Continuity of commitment.

  This is to do with maintaining priorities, consistency, and taking the long view.

- Appoint a change agent.

  That's you.

Stage 2: *Diagnosis of change requirements*

- Understand competitors.

  In your personal context, this might well mean those competing demands on your time and energy, conflicting priorities, and so forth.

- Establish the importance of quality.

  Not only the overall quality of your life or the quality of

● Consider your
organisation structure
and technology.

● Assess the contribution
of better workflow/
systems.

● Consider the need to
develop team working.

● Assess competence and
training needs.

● Analyse culture and
attitudes to change.

● Know what people are
thinking.

● Assess the potential for
making discretionary
effort.

*time spent, but the
importance of doing your
best, and in particular
always doing things in the
best possible way.*

*Are you wasting time – and
therefore money – coping
with an inefficient
typewriter/car/appliance?
Would a redistribution of
time and effort help? Can
you delegate? Is there an
easier or more efficient
way to get things done?*

*There's a much-used quote
about 'a burden shared'.
Balance it against the one
about 'too many cooks'
before finalising your
decision.*

*We're now in the process
of working on these.*

*You know the people
around you as well as
anybody. In some cases
you're the one who knows
them best. How are they
going to react? How will
you deal with their
reactions? And, in
particular, how can you
minimise any negative
reactions?*

*If you don't know, ask. And
then be sure to listen to the
answers.*

*Can you delegate
decisions as well as tasks?*

Stage 3: *Promoting the need for change*

- Justify change.

Be absolutely clear in your own mind what you really want to change, and why it is the right course to take.

- Explain to all 'employees'.

See previous item. Remember, you're the 'boss' – but if, for instance, your kids understand what's going on, they're more likely to co-operate willingly.

- Work with internal 'customers'.

As above. If mealtimes are going to change, make sure that your new catering arrangements are seen to take account of their needs.

- Integrate supplier relations.

Does the supermarket deliver? Or if you're defining 'supplier' as anyone who contributes to your own efforts, make sure they understand your new needs, schedules, etc.

- Work with external 'customers'.

These might be defined as the boss at your new job, actual customers of your own new business, or anyone outside your personal 'company' to whom you're responsible. Gauge to what extent you can enlist their co-operation in adjusting to your personal 'change'.

Stage 4: *Planning the change process*

- Integrate all the elements.

  All of the above should be incorporated into your action plan. How will each role and relationship be affected by the change?

- Make better use of existing resources.

  Time use, delegating, and so forth.

- Identify opportunities for early success.

  If you plan to achieve your goal in stages, each stage accomplished becomes a success, and a cause for celebration.

- Establish realistic timescales.

  Time use again.

- Provide resources for change.

  In other words, you can't move mountains with a dessert spoon – at least, not within a realistic timescale. So have a clear idea what help – or tools or finance – you'll need to accomplish your change, and make sure they're available to you. Otherwise, you will have to adjust your expectations.

Stage 5: *Enabling change*

- Create open communications.

  Your change will affect everyone around you. They'll need to talk about it. So will you. (We'll be working on communication a bit later.)

- Create ownership of change.

  Since your change may affect everyone around you, it will be a good idea to involve them actively in the process. That will allow them to plan for, take credit for, and take pride in their own resultant changes.

Stage 6: *Training for change*

- Train for leadership.

    You are working on that now.

- Develop line and personnel management skills.

    Extend the lessons learned to your 'colleagues'.

- Train all employees.

    This is obvious – if your kids, for instance, are now going to be responsible for doing their own laundry, it's a good idea to teach them to use the washing machine.

Stage 7: *Review and maintenance of the change process*

- Institutionalise the change process.

    So that not only the specific change itself, but the new ways you and your 'company' think about and approach change, are now built into your life. Again, this is an ongoing process which has already started and which will continue throughout our sequence of exercises.

- Train for continuous change.

    Learn and grow.

- Continuously measure performance and review the change programme.

    This goes back to goal setting, prioritising and review. Once

> *accomplished, has your change brought the results you want? If not, why not? What new changes will you need to begin to reach your goals – or is it time to revise your goals?*

Exercise 3: Change management profile

The final exercise in this section builds on all the work you've done so far. Based on all the lists you've made, goals you've set, diaries you've kept, plans you've made and self-assessment exercises you've tried, you should by now have a number of specific ideas about areas in your life you'd like to change. Choose one.

The change you select should be one that you want to take place within the next few weeks. It might be a goal in itself. If your 'A1' goal is also an 'M' (to be achieved within a month), it would be ideal to work through the changes connected with it. Alternatively, you might want to choose an area that must be changed in order to allow one of your 'A' goals to happen. Or perhaps there's an adjustment you need to make in your life in order to cope with a change that you're faced with.

Start a new sheet in your file. At the top write down the *Target Area* that you've selected for changing. Underneath, list your *reasons* for making the change. Then draw up a simple *action plan*, using the Action Planning techniques we tried out in Chapter 3 to set out the tasks or actions that need to be done, when, and by whom, and what resources you'll need. Keep the Managing Change Checklist in mind when deciding what needs to be done. Finally, *prioritise* the list.

Then, over the next few weeks, while you're implementing your change, work through the following questionnaire. Keep written notes throughout to help you monitor your progress.

Before the change

Examine your feelings and expectations.

- Am I anxious about anything? If so, what?
- Am I excited about anything? If so, what?
- What am I looking forward to?
- What will I miss?
- How do I think other people will react?
  What have I done to find out?
- Will there be any difficulties? If so, what?
- Is there anything I can do now to prepare? If so, what?
- What help will be available if I need any? What kind, from where?

During the change

Try each of these coping techniques, where appropriate, and note whether or not it helps.

- Talk through your feelings with somebody. Does it help?
- Find somewhere quiet to relax. Does it help?
- Try thinking about something good that has happened to you. Does it help?
- Do something physical. Does it help? Try others.
- List all the best things about the new situation. Does it help?
- Give yourself a treat – something you really enjoy. Does it help?

Moving through the transition

Think about the following:

- When did I begin to feel relaxed with, or adjusted to, the new situation?
- How long has the transition lasted?
- What helped me to feel better about it?
- What did other people do to help me?
- Are there any differences between:

– What I expected to happen, and
– What actually happened?

Check back over your answers to the first part of this checklist.

What the transition taught me

What did I learn:

- About myself?
- About other people?
- About moving into new situations?

As you continue to work through the exercises in subsequent chapters, return to the notes you've made against each of these points, and monitor any differences as they develop.

6

Identification of skills, aptitudes and abilities – 2

We are now going to face the 'oh it was nothing' syndrome head-on. This is serious business. With a bit of luck and some concentrated effort, we may just eradicate the dreaded phrase from your vocabulary entirely.

In Chapter 1, we spent a good deal of time looking at all the different things you do in the ordinary course of your life. Now the emphasis will shift from what you do, to what that's worth. This chapter is concerned with identifying your skills and abilities, and then valuing them, in terms of both importance to you, and real money value. Realising the worth of these everyday skills can be surprising. It can be an important step in clarifying your hidden potential.

The following three exercises should help you to gain a clearer picture of your skills and abilities, identify skills and abilities you may not have realised you had, and value skills you may not have valued before.

Exercise 1: Skills stocktake

This is a four part exercise.

Step 1

The first part will give you a quick overview of your life so far. Divide your life so far into approximately four manageable

40

segments. The divisions you select should make sense in terms of your own age and experience.

For instance: *up to 18 / 18–30 / 30–45 / 45 onwards* will be suitable if you're in your late fifties. If you're now 23, however, the four segments might be more like *school / secondary school / 16–20 / 21 onwards*. Or you might see the segments in your life dividing according to where you lived at a given period and what you were doing.

Using a separate sheet for each of the four segments, take five minutes to list all the important happenings, qualifications or awards, achievements and main events that occurred during that period. Events might include such things as leaving school, starting work, learning to drive, winning a competition, taking a course, starting (or ending) a relationship, having a baby, and so on.

Note: For the purposes of this exercise, you don't need to explain or justify anything, account for the whole timespan, or try to impress anyone. The things that are most important to you should pop into your mind quickly, and without any effort.

Step 2

Next, make a list of your achievements. Write down ten things you have done. These can include just about any-thing, from any time in your life. Some of them might be things like: cooked a special meal; listened to a friend with troubles; made something; helped to organise an activity or event; learned how to ski; changed your appearance.

Step 3

Choose the eight most important items from Steps 1 and 2. You don't have to list them in any particular order.

Step 4

Take a large ruled sheet of paper. Down the left-hand side, one item per line, list the following skills and abilities: skill with animals; artistic skills; caring; communication; courage/

taking risks; constant hard work; dealing with people; decision-making; efficiency; eye for detail; food skills; ideas; being imaginative; leadership; listening; management; good memory; money skills; patience; reliability; research; self-discipline; solving problems; stamina; tolerance; working with hands; and writing. Add any others you can think of which are relevant to your life.

Next, rule eight vertical columns, and across the top write your eight most important achievements from Step 3 – one at the top of each column (Fig. 6.1). Now work down each column and tick the skills and abilities you think were involved in achieving the item written at the top. There will be several ticks in each column.

For instance, writing a book is quite an achievement. Besides writing, it can involve communication, taking risks, constant hard work, decision-making, eye for detail, ideas and imagination, research, self-discipline, and – especially as the deadline approaches – stamina. Organising a birthday party for a five-year-old might involve artistic skills (gift wrapping and decorations), dealing with people, decision-making, food skills, being imaginative – and, on the day, patience, stamina, and tolerance.

When you've completed your grid, there are two obvious things to look for. Firstly, some of your achievements – perhaps most of them – required a wide range of skills. Pat yourself on the back. (Add athletic ability to your list if you are able to do this physically!)

Secondly, which skills on the list had the most ticks against them? Counting them up may give you an idea of what you naturally do best. Grouping skills together realistically (for example, communication + dealing with people + decision-making + leadership + management) might well suggest a particular direction or occupation. Which of your strongest skills would fit together? What sort of job or profession would require that set of skills? Think about it. Discuss it with friends. Keep it in your file for future reference.

Most important achievements

	1	2	3	4	5	6	7	8
Skill with animals								
Artistic skills								
Caring								
Communication								
Courage/Taking a risk								
Constant hard work								
Dealing with people								
Decision making								
Efficiency								
Eye for detail								
Food skills								
Ideas								
Being imaginative								
Leadership								
Listening								
Management								
Good memory								
Money skills								
Patience								
Reliability								
Research								
Self discipline								
Solving problems								
Stamina								
Tolerance								
Working with hands								
Writing								

Figure 6.1 Skills stocktaking sheet

Exercise 2: Housewife's salary

This exercise is a 'golden oldie'. It is wheeled out regularly in connection with equal opportunity and social security issues, and occasionally in negotiating divorce or insurance settlements. It never fails to amaze all of the various categories of men, in any number of contexts, who tend to undervalue 'women's work'.

As we've said before, if anyone is likely to undervalue a woman's achievements, it's the woman herself. We are therefore going to spend a bit of time putting a realistic price tag on your routine activities.

Refer back to the work you've done so far on roles played and time spent. In particular, you will need to consult the accurate record of one week's time use which you compiled in Chapter 4. Then make a list of all the roles you played during the week you monitored, and after each write the amount of time you spent at it. For example:

cook	14 hours
cleaner	12 hours
washerwoman	6 hours
bookkeeper	1 hour
taxi driver	1 hour
gardener	2 hours
telephonist	½ hour
secretary	1 hour
childminder	45 hours
seamstress	1 hour
tutor	3 hours

and so forth. (This is by no means a complete list – yours will probably be somewhat longer.)

Just adding up the number of hours you're committed to weekly might be interesting, but we're going to take it further. You will have to do a little research next. Find out how much per hour a cook earns in your area. Do the same for cleaners, bookkeepers, and every other role on your list. You may find the information you need from the Situations

Vacant columns in local and national newspapers, adverts in *The Lady*, notices posted at the Job Centre.

When in doubt, use the European minimum wage (approximately £3.40 per hour). If you feel you deserve it (and why not?) list your roles as chef rather than cook, accountant rather than bookkeeper, landscape designer rather than gardener – and give yourself a pay rise. Write in the amounts against each job role. Pay rates vary considerably between regions, and will be especially high in London, but they might be something like the following:

chef	£7.50
cleaner	£2.50
laundress	£2.50
accountant	£8.00
taxi driver	£3.50
landscape designer	£20.00
telephonist	£3.20
secretary	£4.50
childminder	£2.00
seamstress	£3.50
tutor	£9.00

Now get out your calculator and multiply them out:

chef	14 hours	×	£7.50	=	£105.00
cleaner	12 hours	×	£2.50	=	£30.00
laundress	6 hours	×	£2.50	=	£15.00
accountant	1 hour	×	£8.00	=	£8.00
taxi driver	1 hour	×	£3.50	=	£3.50
landscape designer	2 hours	×	£20.00	=	£40.00
telephonist	½ hour	×	£3.20	=	£1.60
secretary	1 hour	×	£4.50	=	£4.50
childminder	45 hours	×	£2.00	=	£90.00
seamstress	1 hour	×	£3.50	=	£3.50
tutor	3 hours	×	£9.00	=	£27.00

Finally, add them all up. The grand total on our partial, hypothetical list is £328.10. That is already pretty impressive – your own week may have a lot more in it. And if you also have a 'real' job, by all means add that in, too. The total represents your commercial replacement value. In crass, financial terms it is what you're worth in an average week.

Exercise 3: Positive profile statement

The final exercise to round off this chapter is simply to write down ten positive statements about yourself. This is not actually very easy. We often find it hard to tell other people what we're good at. (Another manifestation of the 'oh it was nothing' syndrome.) Nevertheless, try. Your Positive Profile Statement might look something like this:

I am someone who:

- is a good cook
- cares for others
- is a good driver
- can handle money
- listens to others
- can instil confidence in others
- can do the ironing well
- can handle illness and injury
- copes with change.

The most important thing to remember is that the statements must be genuinely *positive*. Things like 'I'm good at burning the toast' do not qualify.

If you find you're having trouble with this one, don't give up – there will definitely be ten good things to say about yourself. Look back at the lists of achievements you compiled at the beginning of this chapter. Refer to the brain mapping exercise in Chapter 1. Enlist a little help from your friends – other people can often see our strengths more clearly than we can ourselves. And generally they're happy to say nice (positive) things about us.

When you have come up with your ten positive statements, write them out *nicely* on a clean piece of paper. Put it where you will see it regularly – over your desk, at the front of your diary, on the bathroom mirror. If you get too used to seeing it (in other words, if you find yourself starting to ignore what you've written), repeat the exercise. List ten *more* positive things about yourself. You should find it easier this time.

Positive thinking

All the exercises in this chapter have been designed to get you in the habit of thinking *positively* about yourself and what you've accomplished. The power of positive thinking has been proven so often, it's almost a cliché: it is true, however, that if a door-to-door encyclopaedia salesman sets out in the morning *knowing* that he will sell seven sets that day, he probably will do so. If he goes out thinking 'Oh, no, I can't possibly sell seven of these things', he probably won't reach his target.

It's quite simple, really. If you think you can, you can. Our thinking influences our actions. Our actions influence other people's response to us. We are what we think. People respond to the signals we send out to them which tell them what we are. That is getting into the area of communication, more about which in the next chapter.

There's another old saying that fits nicely here: 'Smile and the world smiles with you . . .' The second half is irrelevant.

7

Communication – 1

Everything we do and say makes a statement about us that is interpreted by others. Sometimes we don't intend to send any message at all. Sometimes the message we send will be what we wanted to express, sometimes not. At other times we get the response we want from others. And occasionally we wonder why people just don't understand us – or why they seem to be so stupid, or aggressive, or totally uninterested. Being able to communicate effectively is vital. In this chapter we're going to look at different ways of communicating, with a view to becoming a more effective communicator.

Exercise 1: How we communicate

Communication can be described simply as 'the passage of ideas and messages'. African talking drums, hunting horns, symbolically engraved medallions sent into space, and traffic lights are all forms of communication. So is an animal marking its territory. All convey ideas, send messages. Speaking, writing, singing, drawing, or choosing to wear a particular style of clothes are all examples of messages that we send deliberately. Involuntary facial expressions or tone of voice send unintentional messages.

In this exercise, we are going to look more closely at various kinds of communication. First, take a large sheet of paper and use it to make a list of as many examples of

48

communication as you can think of. You might list cuddling a child, whistling for the dog, watching television, shaking your fist at a careless driver, raising your eyebrows, gasping in surprise, winking at somebody, writing a letter to apply for a job. The list could be endless, but stop when you've filled a page.

Next classify your list roughly into four main categories of communication:

Spoken communication

Talking, also listening, which is the receiving end of spoken communication. You might extend it to include anything transmitted via an audio medium. It could be a conversation between two people, or a one-sided communication delivered by one person to any number of listeners, as in a political speech, a recorded song, or the patter of the radio DJ who plays it.

Written communication

The written word – all language functions, including codes and made-up languages, that you *look* at rather than hear. Examples are newspaper or magazine articles, leaflets, books, instruction sheets, legal documents, a recipe, or even a musical score.

Visual communication

Signs and symbols (but not words), which you see and then interpret. These might include photographs, styles of clothing, graphics, or the international symbols used In road signs.

Body language

Messages and Ideas transmitted by the way you use your body, either deliberately or unconsciously. Your general bearing can give the impression of timidity, bossiness or confidence, for example. Yawning might suggest boredom, facial expressions convey anger, contempt, hurt, and so forth.

Some of the items on your list will be obvious, others a bit complicated to classify. Music – played or listened to – might be considered an abstract example of spoken communication, even if it's instrumental. A musical score, on the other hand, would come under written communication.

It's interesting to note that some psychologists would classify television as spoken communication, because it uses more audio skills than visual. After much discussion, we concluded that Morse Code is fundamentally an audio (spoken) communication, although generally it's first written and, once received, translated again into written form. Semaphore is highly organised body language.

Exercise 2: Rate yourself

Having given a bit of thought to what constitutes which sort of communication, think about how successful you are at expressing yourself through spoken communication, visual communication, written communication and body language. Starting with the one you're strongest on, and working down to the weakest, how would you rate yourself on each of the four, and why? Think it through carefully. Be honest. For example:

- *Written communication* is my strongest suit – I think I've always had a good understanding of language, and can translate thoughts into words quite easily (especially with the help of a word processor).
- *Visual communication* is less strong – maybe because I concentrate less on it. But I think I'm pretty good at suiting clothes to the mood or occasion, drawing little maps or room layouts that people can understand, and other things like that.
- *Body language* is something that's mostly uncon- scious – so I suppose I have less control of it. On the plus

side, though, if someone in a queue is being ill-mannered, I can sometimes provoke an apology just by throwing them a meaningful look.

- *Spoken communication* is dead last. I'm often perfectly OK at this – but there are times when I just can't get a straight sentence out (usually through shyness or lack of confidence in what I'm trying to say). I also have to admit that occasionally I don't listen properly to what others are saying.

When you have finished rating your own communication abilities, ask yourself these questions: Where are your communication strengths? Where are the weaknesses? Are there areas where you need to build up a little muscle? If so, the following exercises might help.

Exercise 3: Every little movement has a meaning

At least once per romance, the fictional heroine will be betrayed by her body. She blushes, she trembles, she can't help reaching out and touching him. Fortunately for the course of true love, her body language conveys her real feelings to the dashing hero, and he takes appropriate action.

Similar things happen in real life, although not always with such thrilling consequences. You're at a job interview, you're cool, calm, intelligent – and you're unconsciously tearing a tissue to shreds. Or, 'Oh, how lovely. Just what I've always wanted,' you state enthusiastically – but your forced smile doesn't quite hide the look of distaste. Or, you're trying to explain something really important to your husband, who nods and occasionally makes interested noises – but he also yawns and keeps looking at his watch.

Because much of body language is unconscious, it's the hardest form of communication to control – or to fake. In fact, care workers on psychiatric wards are instructed that if ever there's a conflict between what a patient says and does, always to believe the physical signs. (Saying something like 'I'm your friend' whilst shaking a clenched fist, is

51

one example.) Body language experts can watch video tapes of, for instance, politicians and analyse their eye movements to determine when they're lying.

In more ordinary circumstances, we all naturally send out unconscious signals, and people on the receiving end become aware of the conflicting messages, even if it's just an 'impression' or 'feeling'. What can you do about it? Just by becoming more aware of what you are doing, you can begin to modify your own responses. For a day or two, keep a 'body language' diary, taking particular note of unconscious responses from the people around you. Keep notes on:

- What was the situation?
- What was the *body language* reaction?
- What did it mean to you?

Follow this up with some self-observation along the same lines, this time gauging other people's response to you, and trying to identify what it is that *triggers* your involuntary reactions. Understanding what is happening to you is the first step towards anticipating, and then being able to control your reactions.

Exercise 4: Sit right down and write

Written communication, on the other hand, is usually the most deliberate, and therefore should be most easily controlled. If you write a message and get it wrong, you can simply rewrite it. If you read a book and don't understand it, you can read it more slowly, read it again, look up words you don't understand, or even ask somebody else to explain it.

List three things you've written and then rewritten in the past week. For each of them, note its purpose, why you chose to write it down in the first place, and why you rewrote it. An example might be a shopping list; its purpose is a reminder to use at the supermarket; you wrote it because it's easy to check and easy to remember; and you rewrote it because you needed to add some items and had already bought others.

Rewriting is vital when you need to get your message across to somebody clearly, and when you want to give them the correct impression. To demonstrate, try writing a simple note to change an appointment. Obviously, it's important to state the facts correctly and clearly (time, date, place, etc), so that there will be no possibility of misunderstanding. But how would you send the identical factual information to:

- a close friend;
- your boss;
- a prospective employer;
- the vicar;
- your child's teacher;
- your dentist; or
- the Queen?

It's pretty obvious that no two of these letters will be the same. They'll differ in tone, length, language, even the amount or type of information you find it necessary to include (for instance, the reason for the change, an apology, how you feel about it all, and so forth).

Exercise 5: I wish I'd said that

Sometimes it's possible to plan what we say in advance. If we are going to give a speech, for instance, it may well involve written preparation as well as practising voice control, expression and performance. More often than not, though, we find ourselves wishing we'd thought just a bit more before opening our mouths. Think of a recent instance when that happened to you, and then answer the following questions:

- What was the situation?
- What prompted you to say what you did?
- What did you actually say?

- What was the result of this communication?
- With hindsight, what could you have said or done to make the result better for you?

The best ways to control spoken communication are to try and anticipate what is likely to happen in a situation, decide what you want to achieve from the communication, or try to slow the communication down so that you can respond effectively.

Exercise 6: Do you see what I see?

An enormous amount of thought can go into visual communication. Advertising images are carefully planned to create a particular (sometimes subliminal) impression. Companies might spend millions to develop the perfect logo. Symbols, such as traffic lights and roadsigns, are used to deliver messages clearly and quickly. The international symbol of a red circle with diagonal bar (below) superimposed on a recognisable picture of something is recognised to mean 'Do not' in any language.

 **NO SMOKING**    **NO DOGS**

Figure 7.1

The 'Do Not' symbols combined with pictographs such as a lit cigarette or a dog (meaning 'No Smoking' and 'Dogs Not Allowed', respectively) are obvious. They're easily recognised and fulfil their universal communication function perfectly. In December, a local cafe used to post signs with the barred circle superimposed on a picture of Santa Claus. This clearly indicated a 'Christmas-free Zone' where you could expect business as usual, despite the season.

Of course, this kind of visual information presupposes a certain level of understanding from the viewer. The signs below may well signal 'Men's' and 'Women's' toilet facilities, but you have to know that the Ladies is available to all women, not just those with one leg!

GENTS   **LADIES**

Figure 7.2

Exercise 7: First impressions

What people look like is another form of visual communication – this involves a subtle combination of their physical features, what they wear, plus their speech and body language. People send out signals – both deliberately and unconsciously – and other people make snap judgments about them, based largely on an instinctive interpretation of those signals.

Imagine that you are in the arrivals hall at Gatwick, with a bit of time to observe the people around you. Based solely on the *visual* communication signalled by the way they chose to dress, what do your instincts tell you about these people:

A Purple hair, black ripped jeans, black vest T-shirt, Doc Martin boots.

B Twinset, tweed skirt, pearls, wavy hair, a little lipstick.

C Navy suit, black well-polished shoes, white shirt, blue tie.

D Short hair, moustache, trainers, jogging suit.

E Corduroy trousers, check shirt, tweed jacket, untidy hair, pipe.

F Well-styled hair, dress with shoulder pads, high heels, stockings with seams, full make-up.

You probably had no trouble making a quick judgement about who our six friends might be. Unfortunately, because you've had limited information, your instinctive character appraisals may have been a bit off the mark. Time drags on, and they start to chat amongst themselves. With the added information on their *spoken* communication, now who do you think they are:

A Purple hair, black ripped jeans, black vest T-shirt, Doc Martin boots. Speaks in a quiet voice, with an educated accent, but stammers.

B Twinset, tweed skirt, pearls, wavy hair, a little lipstick. Has an extremely brisk and abrupt way of speaking. Gives a lot of orders.

C Navy suit, black well-polished shoes, white shirt, blue tie. Speaks very quickly and loudly. Has a strong London accent. Tells bad jokes and laughs at them.

D Short hair, moustache, trainers, jogging suit. Has a rough voice, inner city accent and hostile tone of voice.

E Corduroy trousers, check shirt, tweed jacket, untidy hair, pipe. Strong country accent, very slow of speech.

F Well-styled hair, dress with shoulder pads, high heels, stockings with seams, full make-up. Strong coarse accent from an undefined big town. Talks with a low, slow voice.

Surprising, isn't it? Could you answer the following questions about these people, based on what you've observed so far?

- Are they married or single?

- What type of car do they drive?

- Where were they educated?

- Do they have children – if so, how many and how old?
- What sort of house do they live in?
- How is it decorated?
- How do they vote?
- What do they drink?
- What do they do in their free time?
- What do they do for a living?
- Where do they go on holiday?
- Who are they meeting? Describe their respective wives, husbands, girlfriends or boyfriends.

If these were real people, and you were able to observe such things as their body language, the content of their conversations and how they react to each other, your picture of them would be more complete, and your assessment might be a bit fairer. But you might still be surprised at who they met.

You are forgiven for thinking in stereotypes. Most people would. And remember, what this exercise is about is not just how you see others – it's also about how they see you. Which is why it's important to understand how to 'edit' the signals we give out.

Having worked through the exercises in this chapter, you should be able to appreciate that communication is a complex interaction. Some of it is within your control, some is completely outside your control. Much of it can be managed if you are aware of your own and others' reactions.

8

Assertiveness

Some people seem to sail through life getting everything they want without obvious effort. The rest of us have to work at it. What can we do to put our point across, or achieve the result we want from a situation, without upsetting other people or ourselves? What do those 'lucky' people have that we don't have? Assertiveness.

Now, assertiveness training is high on the women's issues agenda. It is frequently linked in people's minds (and sometimes in their experience) with women's self-defence classes, and might therefore conjure up visions of angry feminists in karate gear preparing to do battle to protect their rights. Don't be put off – the fact is, you don't have to deck youself out in any sort of mental combat suit.

Assertiveness is not a martial art, and anyone can use the techniques successfully, regardless of personality. Knowing how to be assertive is not only useful in situations where there is a strong possibility of disagreement, but it can even be used to *prevent* awkward situations.

A quick illustration

You are in a crowded cafe, and as you are about to pour yourself that much-needed cup of tea, you notice that the cup is dirty. Setting aside how long it takes to get the waitress's attention, and how badly you need the tea, you might say:

58

'I beg your pardon, I'm really sorry to trouble you, I don't usually complain about anything, but I'm afraid this cup seems to be a bit dirty, and would you mind terribly much getting me a clean one, please – if it's not too much bother.'

This is *submissive* behaviour. You are inviting the waitress to say 'no' or to take another 40 minutes to get back to you with a clean cup. Alternatively, you might say:

'Oy! This cup is disgusting! I want another one! Now!'

This is *aggressive* behaviour. The waitress might get you a clean cup, or she might get the manager, and you might get thrown out of the cafe.

In reality, this is a cut and dried case. You are entirely in the right. All you have to do is, quite neutrally, point to the facts and state your requirements:

'Excuse me. My cup is dirty. Could you
bring me a clean one, please?'

That is *assertive* behaviour. If it doesn't work, it's the waitress's problem, not yours.

Bill of rights

The key to getting what you want from life – and from other people – lies to a great extent within yourself. To convince others, you first have to convince yourself that everyone, including *you*, has the right:

- to be treated with respect
- to be taken seriously
- to have your own feelings and communicate them
- to be listened to
- to say no – without feeling guilty
- to set your own priorities
- to ask for what you want
- to make mistakes.

You also have the right not to be assertive all the time.

That list of fundamental personal rights, drawn from Anne Dickson's *Assertiveness and You*, is the foundation on which much assertiveness training is built. Life's smooth sailors seem to have an innate belief in those rights. People treat them – and their needs, feelings and ideas – with respect, because they respect themselves, *and it shows*.

Exercise 1: Are you assertive?

How do you feel about doing each of the following?

- *Positive*: Asking a favour; paying a compliment; receiving a compliment; stating a preference; starting a conversation; expressing thanks; giving orders; receiving orders.

- *Negative*: Showing annoyance; showing hurt.

- *Standing up for your rights*: Stating an opinion; voicing a complaint; saying no.

Most of us would answer 'It depends.' You probably feel differently doing each of the above vis-à-vis different sorts of people, for instance: a child, your partner, parent, friend, brother or sister, a bank manager or official, a salesman, a shop assistant or waitress, a handyman, a stranger.

Fill in the grid in figure 8.1 by marking each with a tick if you can do it easily, a cross if you find it difficult, and a question mark if you're not sure. When you've finished, count up the number of ticks.

Assertiveness techniques

The impression you want to give when you're being assertive is one of firmness and authority. There are any number of techniques to help you do this. Most of them centre on planning ahead, believing in what you're fighting for, and using good communication skills.

POSITIVE:	Child	Partner	Parent	Friend	Brother/ Sister	Bank Mgr/ Official	Sales-man	Shop assistant/ Waitress	Handy-man	Stranger
Asking a favour										
Paying a compliment										
Receiving a compliment										
Stating a preference										
Starting a conversation										
Expressing thanks										
Giving orders										
Receiving orders										
NEGATIVE:										
Showing annoyance										
Showing hurt										
STANDING UP FOR YOUR RIGHTS: Stating an opinion										
Voicing a complaint										
Saying no										

Figure 8.1 Assessing assertiveness

Planning is important because:

- You can check your facts beforehand to make sure they're absolutely correct.
- You can assess whether your case is valid and worth pursuing.
- You can practise what you're going to say until you feel comfortable with it.

To be assertive, you need to put your ideas across in a well-thought out way.

Believing in your case is important because:

- The people you'll be dealing with may be only too willing to point out why they disagree.
- If you start to think your position might be unreasonable, it's very easy to become intimidated and lapse into non-assertive behaviour.
- You'll be able to take a positive attitude to what you're doing.

You need to stay calm and in control. A negative attitude will colour your communication, giving the advantage to the other person.

Good communication is important because:

- You need to say exactly what you mean.
- You need to know how to stand your ground and counter disagreement.
- You need to be sure of exactly what a person means when they answer you.
- You may need to keep repeating your key points until they sink in.
- You should aim for a definite outcome to the conversation – a 'maybe' may mean you'll have to repeat the process.

This list might go on to include everything covered in Chapter 7 (qv).

Exercise 2: Assertiveness practice

The only way to practise assertiveness is to be assertive. But before launching yourself on an unsuspecting public, you might want to do a bit of work in private. First, work through the following hypothetical cases.

Case study: Marjorie

Marjorie has recently taken out a year's contract to hire a video recorder. She is not happy with the machine she has been given: the picture is not clear, it's not a good quality machine. The company she hired it from has been running a promotion offering a much better quality machine for the same price.

Marjorie would like to change her machine for the one being promoted. She goes back to the shop to ask if she can. The assistant is not helpful, and says that the better machine is only available to new customers, and anyway they have run out of them at that branch. Marjorie does not mention the poor quality picture she is getting. She gets home feeling cross with herself. She decides to go back and be assertive.

Answer the following questions:
1. What should she do to prepare?
2. What does she want to achieve?
3. What facts does she need to check?
4. What are the pros and cons of her argument?
5. What grounds has she got for negotiation? What are the strengths of her case?
6. What are the weaknesses of her case?
7. What are the strengths of the shop's case?
8. What are the weaknesses of the shop's case?
9. How should she approach the staff in the shop?
10. What could her opening line be?
11. What are their arguments likely to be?
12. What do you think she will achieve?

Case study: Joan

Joan has just started working as an accounts clerk. Her job is to process invoices for payment and enter them on a computer. She frequently has to deal with suppliers' queries about when they'll be paid, but it isn't really part of her job, and beyond checking whether they've been entered on the computer, she doesn't know much about it.

Tanya is the head bookkeeper. She is a whiz with accounts, but doesn't seem to like dealing with people. She isn't interested in the suppliers' problems, and often doesn't issue payments automatically once they've been entered. The Chief Accountant is based at Head Office, and isn't available to sort out day-to-day difficulties.

Several times Joan has had to deal with irate suppliers who haven't received cheques by the date they'd been told to expect payment. Tanya refuses to deal with the suppliers directly, and sends excuses to them via Joan. Joan is fed up with being 'piggy-in-the-middle'. She feels like leaving the job. Could she make her situation better by using assertive behaviour?

Answer the following questions:

1. What do you think Joan wants to achieve?
2. With which people does Joan need to be assertive?
3. What facts does Joan need to check?
4. What are the pros and cons of her argument?
5. What grounds has she got for negotiation? What are the strengths of her case? What factors in the situation are likely to work in her favour?
6. What are the weaknesses of her case? What factors in the situation are likely to work against her?
7. What are the strengths and weaknesses of Tanya's position?
8. What are the strengths and weaknesses of the Chief Accountant's position?
9. What are the strengths and weaknesses of the suppliers' case?
10. Who should Joan approach first?
11. What could her approach be?

12. What is this person's argument likely to be?
13. What should Joan's counter-argument be?
14. If this doesn't work, what should her next move be?
15. How should she approach this next move, bearing in mind what experience she might have gained from her previous approach?
16. What do you think she will achieve?

There are no right or wrong answers to these questions. The important thing is to think through the approaches to different people and situations in order to try and achieve your goal. The following are examples of possible answers.

In Marjorie's case, you might have decided that the strength of her case was that she had a machine that was not working properly. Therefore she was entitled to a replacement. The weakness in her case might be that she was not entitled to have the machine replaced by the model she wanted. Therefore she would have to be assertive to get her own way over this.

In Joan's case you might have said that she could point out to the Chief Accountant that relations with their suppliers and therefore production might suffer if Tanya continued acting this way. The result might be that if she got the boss on her side, Tanya might become even more difficult to work with, or even leave – and maybe keeping a good book-keeper is more important to the Chief Accountant than an accounts clerk or a particular supplier, or maybe he just wouldn't want to be bothered.

If you find yourself in a difficult situation, you may find it useful to think things through in this way, so that you can anticipate other people's reactions and be prepared to put forward your case assertively.

Exercise 3: Mirror, mirror

You might want to practise assertiveness techniques in private. Some people find it useful to try things out in front of their mirror; others use tape recorders; a time-honoured technique is to go to an isolated stretch of beach and shout at the surf. Work on your tone of voice, facial expression, body language, and choice of words. You might also find it useful to enlist the help of a sympathetic friend or family member to practise role playing in a variety of situations.

Step 1

Whether you're working alone or with someone, you can try out your technique on the following:

Situation 1   Returning an unsatisfactory meal.

Situation 2   Refusing to do an unreasonable favour.

Situation 3   Returning an unwanted purchase.

Step 2

Try the same three situations again, but this time from the other person's point of view:

Situation 1   You're the waitress, the meal is not that bad, and it might come out of your pay.

Situation 2   You're really desperate, and what are friends for?

Situation 3   You're the manager, and the shop has an absolute policy of not allowing refunds unless the goods are badly defective.

Exercise 4: The real thing

If you haven't yet applied what you've learned about assertiveness in real life situations, now is the time to try. First, without trying too much to change your behaviour, just observe yourself in action for a day or two. Keep notes (mental notes, if you prefer) and then analyse two or three situations and note how you acted. Were you submissive, aggressive or assertive? Then decide whether your behaviour might need to be changed and, if so, what you will do to change it.

When you find yourself in situations where you need to be assertive, remember: *plan, believe in what you want to achieve*, and *use good communication skills*. Keep trying until you're satisfied that you're getting the responses you want. Then have a go at applying assertiveness techniques to the change you selected in Chapter 5.

Remember: You want to be able to think 'I will say or do that . . .' not 'I wish I had said or done something else'.

9

Relationships, expectations, and everyday transactions

Women have come a long way in the past two or three decades. Of course, there's still a lot of work to be done – both individually and en masse. But it's clear that our chances are better than ever to be listened to, to be taken seriously, to make our own choices, to take advantage of opportunities, and to take responsibility for our own lives. Our improved status is intimately connected with the progress that's been made in the ways people perceive relationships.

For an especially clear demonstration of how far the world has come, try to catch a Hollywood 'romantic comedy' of the early 1960s next time one is re-run on television. From the perspective of the nineties those movies seem neither romantic nor comic – certainly not in terms of how they portrayed relationships between adult men and women.

One film which leaps to mind in this context starred Bobby Darin and Sandra Dee as a couple who fell in love and got married. (This was considered innovative casting at the time, because in real life Bobby and Sandra had recently fallen in love and got married.) In the movie, however, they did not live happily ever after. They were miserable, fighting, forever at cross purposes – until Sandra Dee's mother in the film gave her the little book which saved her marriage.

We are luckier than Sandra Dee. Since the early sixties, much work has been done – and hundreds of books written – on the subjects of communication and relationships. Anyone who wants help these days can buy a book, phone an advice line, read all about it in women's magazines, hear all about it on daytime chat shows. You don't even have to be married to visit a marriage counsellor. But all poor Sandra had to go on was a little illustrated manual on how to train your pet dog. Needless to say, it worked. (This was, after all, a Hollywood movie.) The moral of the film seemed to be that if you treat your husband like a pet poodle, he will trot happily along at your heel, and you will live happily ever after.

Appalling as it is to admit, this approach is less far-fetched than it might seem on the face of it. Any discerning fan of Barbara Woodhouse's dog training programme will testify that her techniques were designed to modify the *owner's* behaviour rather than the dog's. Once Miss Woodhouse had the owners well trained, so that they were confident enough to communicate all the right signals, their dogs quickly became perfectly obedient and well-behaved.

The common theme which links Sandra Dee, Barbara Woodhouse and many of the current psychological self-help books on human interaction, might be stated as follows:

- if you understand what happens when you deal with people, at the very least you will probably feel more confident about what is happening;
- if you are more confident, you should as a result be able to deal with them better; and
- if you modify your own behaviour, people are likely to modify their responses to you.

In this chapter you're first going to take a quick look at how you relate to the various people in your life. We'll then explore what happens in everyday transactions: you'll analyse some of your transactions to begin to understand what happens and why, and then begin to alter these transactions – if and when you wish to – by altering your own response.

Exercise 1: Sociograms

We have all sorts of relationships in life. Some deeply involve us emotionally and otherwise, some hardly merit our attention. Some are good, some bad, and most of them will change as our lives change. Some of our relationships are satisfying, some are not.

In order to investigate what makes relationships satisfying or dissatisfying to you, the first step is to take an objective look at those you have at present. You can do this quite easily by drawing a *sociogram* – a simple diagram of the people in your life, and how you relate to them. The following example will give you an idea what a sociogram might look like and how to interpret it:

- Ann lives with her husband, Michael, and her son, Paul. She gets on well with them, but her relationship with Elaine (her sister-in-law, who lives next door) is sometimes good and sometimes bad.
- Ann's closest friend is Mary, and she spends a lot of time with her. Unfortunately, Mary's next-door neighbour Jo is usually there, too. Ann dislikes Jo.
- Ann is very fond of her mother. However, Mother now lives in Canada so their communication is limited to frequent letters, occasional telephone calls, and perhaps one visit in two years.
- Mark is Ann's ex-husband. The marriage ended badly, and she rarely sees him now.
- Ann's Uncle George and Aunt Sarah call in to see them nearly every week, and although she loves to see her Uncle, she finds her Aunt overbearing and critical, and dreads her visits.

Ann's sociogram – setting out all the above in the form of a simple diagram – would look like the one in figure 9.1.

Step 1

Draw your own sociogram. Start by drawing a horizontal line across the middle of a sheet of paper, and then write your name at the centrepoint of the line. Your satisfying relationships will be entered above the line, and unsatisfying relationships below.

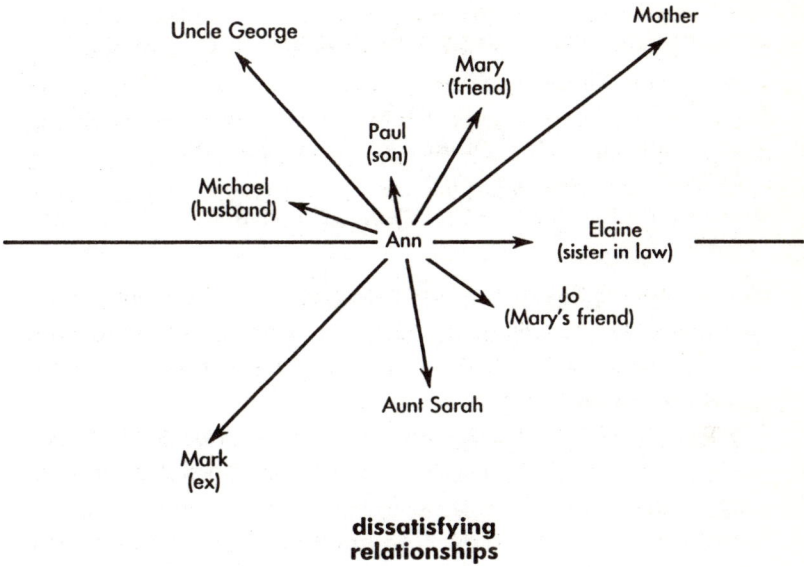

Figure 9.1 Anne's sociogram

Draw lines radiating out from your name (like spokes on a wheel) to represent each relationship you're currently involved in. Use a short line to indicate that the person named is one you meet or talk to frequently. The longer the line, the further away they are from you (but not necessarily geographically), and the less communication you have with them.

For this exercise, your sociogram only needs to be as simple as the example given. However, if you find the exercise especially interesting, you could develop it further using symbols, colours, arrows, and so forth, to create a quite elaborate diagram.

Step 2

Analysis. Using your sociogram as a prompt, think about each of your relationships. What is it about the way each

71

person behaves towards you, and the way you behave towards him or her, that makes the relationship satisfying or not? For each relationship, list the following:

- Things that the other person does that make the relationship satisfying.
- Things that you do that make the relationship satisfying.
- Anything that the other person does that makes the relationship dissatisfying.
- Anything that you do that makes the relationship dissatisfying.

Be as specific as you can. For instance, don't limit your notes to things like 'She's a good friend'. Instead, write 'She listens when I have a problem' or 'She makes me laugh when I'm down'.

When you've worked through each name on your sociogram, try to draw some general conclusions from the notes you've made. Draw up a list of those things that you believe help relationships, and another of those that hinder relationships.

Remember: Relationships don't just happen – they have to be worked at. Even when they start off well, relationships continue to be satisfying only if both people involved do things to help the relationship (refer to your list).

Exercise 2: Expectations

Expectations play a key part in how relationships prosper. To take a very simple example: if you *expect* to meet a friend for lunch, and she doesn't show up, how do you feel? Angry? Let down? Unimportant? We naturally expect that other people will keep to agreements and arrangements we've made with them. But living up to unspoken agreements can be equally – if not more – important to the well-being of our relationships.

Think of a time recently when you have felt 'let down' by someone.

- Write a brief description of what happened, who said or did what, and to whom.
- What had you *expected* the other person to do or say that was different from what actually happened?
- Do you think the other person knew what you expected?
- List all the reasons you can think of why s/he said or did what s/he said or did.

How can you begin to understand what people do and why? You might consider having deep, searching conversations with everyone you know in order to analyse the inner meaning of every interaction you have with them. This is not a recommended technique, however – it's more likely to undermine your relationships than to sort them out. The best alternative in your quest for understanding of these interactions is simply to ask *yourself* a few basic questions:

- Why am I feeling like this?
- What did I expect the other person to do or say differently?
- Does the other person know about my expectations?
- Is it reasonable to expect this of the other person?

It's healthy to remember that everybody has their own problems. People often do or say things to you for reasons which have little or nothing to do with you – just as you may react the way you do for reasons which have little or nothing to do with them. With that in mind, we'll move on to the central subject of this chapter.

Transactional Analysis

In the beginning there was Freud, whose approach to human behaviour can be summed up (far too simply) in two short sentences:

'Men only want one thing'

and

'What do women want?'

73

Freud never did find a satisfactory answer to the latter. Fortunately for women, since Freud there have been a number of useful developments in the study of how people relate to one another. Arguably the most talked-about approach of the past few decades is Transactional Analysis.

Transactional Analysis was popularised largely through the work of two psychologists: Eric Berne ('Games People Play') and Thomas A. Harris ('I'm OK – You're OK'). The part of their theories which we are going to work on now can be stated roughly as follows:

> Whenever two people talk to each other, the Sender will stimulate and activate one of the three parts in the Receiver's nature. These three ego states are the 'Child', the 'Parent', and the 'Adult'. If you understand which part of you is triggered in everyday transactions, it can help you to alter your response where necessary, to allow communication to flow freely.

From the minute we're born, we begin to receive messages and collect information, first from our parents and later from others. These transactions are recorded in our brains or minds as a sort of immense 'database'. Depending on how these messages were first sent and received, the data stored may be 'contaminated'. Where that has happened, there are likely to be blocks in how we respond to similar messages later in life.

The Parent in you is a database of straight, unquestioned commands, rules and laws delivered mainly by parents, and later by other authority figures. When your *Parent* ego state is active, you are in effect either quoting or obeying your parents.

The Child in you is a database of responses and feelings – generally your uncensored internal reactions to what you saw and heard. These feelings can be either positive ('I'm OK') or negative ('I'm not OK'). When your responses are emotional, the *Child* ego state has taken over.

The Adult in you is the processor which organises all those bits of information stored in your Child and Parent databases. It is a database of what you found out and tested for yourself, as opposed to what you were taught, or what you felt or wished. The *Adult* ego state is able to look at the Parent and Child data,

74

determine whether it's true, and then decide whether to accept or reject it.

Exercise 3: Ego states

Step 1

Rule three columns on a sheet of paper, headed 'Parent', 'Adult', and 'Child'. Sort the following words and phrases into the appropriate columns:

accept, always, analyse, anger, automatic, balance, bossy, censor, command, correction, creativity, curiosity, decide, demand, discipline, discord, efficient, explore, fantasy, feel, frustration, harmony, helpless, how to, ideas, inconsistency, inhibit, insist, instinct, I want, judge, life saver, logic, loving, manageable, manager, mediate, mine is better, never, obedient, order, orderly, play, prefer, reasonable, rebellion, require, rigid, rules, spontaneous, sulky, supposed to, test, uncensored, understanding, wish, who-what-where-when-why.

Step 2

Add any further words and phrases that you can think of to each of the three columns.

Step 3

Think about the associations attached to each of the qualities you've listed as belonging to each of the three ego states. Are these qualities positive or negative? In other words, are they 'OK' or 'Not OK'? Mark them accordingly on your list.

There should be 'OK' and 'Not OK' words in all three lists. Clearly, people aren't supposed to operate from the Adult ego state all the time. Far from it. There are advantages and disadvantages to the qualities expressed by all three of the ego states.

For instance, operating from the Parent ego state (which does things because 'that's the way it's done') can save you an enormous amount of time – you don't need to get bogged down every time in carefully reasoned decisions about what to do and how. The Parent ego state, therefore, would be particularly useful in the armed forces, or in dealing with a large but routine workload. On the other hand, the Child ego state may bring such things as charm, spontaneity, pleasure and creativity to your life.

Everyday transactions

Consider the following illustrations.

You are waiting for a bus. The elderly pensioner sitting next to you grimaces in disapproval at the antics of several teenagers with ghetto-blasters, who are also waiting. The pensioner says:

'Young people today have no manners.'

This is a Parent-to-Parent statement. If your reply were:

'I don't know what the world is coming to'

that would be a Parent-to-Parent reply. This is an example of a complementary transaction, which would be diagrammed as shown in figure 9.2. When the lines are parallel, you can carry on all day without saying anything meaningful. If, on the other hand, your reply were:

'Mind your own business, you old hag'

that is a Child-to-Parent reply, which would simply serve to reinforce the pensioner's belief, and destroy any chance of a reasonable transaction.
However, if you were to say something like:

'I suppose they're a bit irritating, but they're
not doing any real harm, are they?'

76

instigator   **reply**

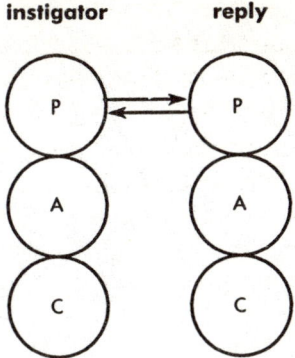

Figure 9.2 Parent-to-Parent reply

that would be an Adult-to-Adult reply. You might get the other person to think a bit. The transaction could alter and improve.

Another example. You are a mother, and you say to your teenaged daughter:

'Go clean up your room.'

This is obviously an appropriate use of the Parent-to-Child communication. If your daughter's reply is 'Yes, Mum' she's clearly replying in an obedient Child-to-Parent mode. The lines are parallel, and you can continue (peacefully) *ad infinitum*. If she says 'Oh, Mum, do I have to?' this is the rebellious Child-to-Parent mode, also parallel, and you can continue (less peacefully) *ad infinitum*. If, however, she says:

'It's my room, you have no right to tell me what to do'

her reply is Parent-to-Child. The transaction is diagrammed in figure 9.3. Communications stop when lines are crossed.

In our third illustration, you tell your small son to eat his porridge (Parent-to-Child). He says 'No! I hate it! You're a horrible cook!' (Child-to-Parent). If you then say 'Right. I'm going to leave and you can cook your own food' – your reply is also Child-to-Parent. Your reaction, whilst understandable, is

mother   **daughter**

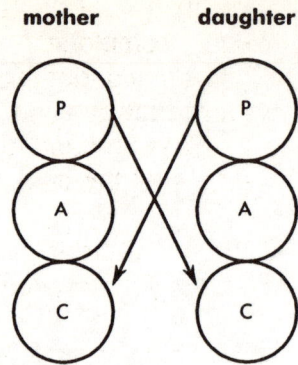

Figure 9.3 Parent-to-Child reply

entirely emotional. At this stage communications are crossed, and you've reached an impasse. Further communication which is at all productive is highly unlikely.

Remember: Our responses in one ego state or another are easily triggered by another person. As we've seen, there are times when any of the three ego states are useful and appropriate. That said, more often than not it's probably preferable to stay in the adult ego state. Unfortunately, having started later than the other two states, the adult state is harder to maintain. Most of us need practice.

When we're uncomfortable about our response, when communications break down, and when we wish we had acted differently – we may be able to respond differently if we understand what is happening inside us.

Exercise 4: Analysing transactions

Analyse the following transactions between a supervisor and her employee. In each case, which ego states did the supervisor initiate, and which ego states were operating in the employee's reply?

1. Supervisor: This report is driving me crazy.
                    Will you help me with it?
    Employee: I don't really have time. Can't you do
                    it yourself?

2. Supervisor: When will you have the balance sheet completed?

    Employee: I know it's due soon, and as you know I always finish it on time.
                    There is no need for you to check up on me all the time.

3. Supervisor: You did a great job on this display.
    Employee: Thank you very much.

4. Supervisor: Why did you go to Mr Smith with this question?

    Employee: I was just trying to do the right thing.

5. Supervisor: Will you work overtime tonight?
    Employee: Why me? Can't you find somebody else?

6. Supervisor: I hate the new policy, but there's nothing I can do about it.

    Employee: I wish you would try a little harder on it.

7. Supervisor: Let's stop at the pub after work.
    Employee: Super!

8. Supervisor: I've done all I can to get good people around here, but it's so difficult to find them.

    Employee: They can't even find reliable kids to deliver the papers.

Answers

1. Supervisor: Child-to-Parent
    Employee: Parent-to-Child
2. Supervisor: Adult-to-Adult
    Employee: Parent-to-Child
3. Supervisor: Adult-to-Adult
    Employee: Adult-to-Adult

79

4. Supervisor: Child-to-Parent
   Employee: Parent-to-Child
5. Supervisor: Adult-to-Adult
   Employee: Child-to-Parent
6. Supervisor: Child-to-Parent
   Employee: Parent-to-Child
7. Supervisor: Child-to-Child
   Employee: Child-to-Child
8. Supervisor: Parent-to-Parent
   Employee: Parent-to-Parent

Exercise 5: Transactions practice

Step 1

How would you respond to each of the following transactions in each of the three ego states?

- You've been sitting for some time in the crowded waiting room at your local Health Centre. The receptionist announces that the doctor has only just arrived, and will now start seeing people in order of appointments. The woman sitting next to you fidgets, sighs, looks at her watch, catches your eye and says:

  'Late again. The NHS is not what it used to be.'

Which ego state is she operating from? What could your response be as Parent, as Child, and as Adult?

- You arrive home from work and find your husband slumped in a chair, looking miserable. He is sick, has a fever and wants attention. He coughs deliberately, sighs loudly, and says, plaintively:

  'My throat hurts. Can I have some tea with honey?'

Which ego state is he operating from? What could your response be as Parent, as Child, and as Adult?

• You and your husband are about to leave for an adult cocktail party, to which your teenaged daughter has also been invited. She comes down stairs wearing patched jeans and a T-shirt. You say:

> 'You can't go to the party looking like that.'

Which ego state are you operating from? What could her response be as Parent, as Child, and as Adult?

• You, your husband and son are camping. You arrive at the campsite near the beach. Your husband is anxious to put up the tent before going swimming. He says to your son:

> 'The first thing you've got to do
> is help me put up the tent.'

Which ego state is he operating from? What could your son's response be as Parent, as Child, and as Adult?

Step 2

As the exercise above demonstrates, everyday situations can be loaded with transactions which trigger our responses from Adult, Child or Parent ego states. Depending on how we respond, these transactions can be 'complementary' or 'parallel', allowing communication to continue; or transactions can sometimes be crossed, resulting in a breakdown in communications.

Practising our responses can enable us to change the transaction, where appropriate, and to get points across *assertively*.

• Review the exercises in Chapter 8.
• Be aware of the dangers of falling into old patterns.

Step 3

Finally, over the next few days, act as an observer. Follow one situation at home or at work: it may be between two neighbours, two members of the family, or between a supervisor and employee. Analyse the transactions that occur between the two people involved. Keep notes, and diagram their interactions using the Adult-Child-Parent model.

- What ego states are operating in each transaction?
- Do you see a pattern in their interactions?
- How else might they have responded to one another in the situation?
- What might have happened differently if one or both had responded differently? How would the outcome of the transaction have changed?

In Chapter 10 we'll apply our observations on relationships and transactions to some further exercises designed to improve how we communicate.

10

Communication – 2

Do you remember playing a children's party game called 'Rumours' or 'Chinese Whispers'? We'd gather in a circle, and one of us whispered a message into the ear of the next child. The message continued to be passed around the circle from one child to the next, until it reached the one who'd started it. Of course the message received was never anything like the message sent – and we always found the distortion hilarious.

As adults we often forget the lesson we learned in the children's game: getting a message correctly from sender to receiver is not necessarily a straightforward proposition.

In the last three chapters, we've worked on various aspects of the complex interactions involved in communication. You've been observing yourself and others as senders and as receivers of messages.

Exercise 1: Recall

Think of a time when you communicated with others, and the message you intended to send either wasn't understood or didn't have the effect you intended. Then answer the following questions:

- What was your intended message?
- What was the message actually received?

- Why do you think the receiver got the wrong message?
- What was the result of the misunderstanding?

Think of a time when you received a message clearly and correctly. Answer the following questions:

- What was the message?
- What method of communication did the sender use?
- What did the sender do to make the message very clear to you?

Think of a time when you *didn't* understand a message. Answer the following questions:

- What was the message?
- What method of communication did the sender use?
- Why do you think you did not understand the message?
- What do you think the sender could have done to communicate the message more effectively?

Exercise 2: Sending

When you are the sender of messages, you are aiming for two things: to have your message clearly understood by the receiver; and to get the reaction you want from the receiver. How can you ensure results? You want to have as much of the following information as possible:

The situation: Who is the receiver likely to be? In what context will the message be delivered? What impression needs to be given?

The content: What are the facts? What information needs to be put across?

The outcome: What do you want to happen or be decided as a result of the communication?

Your attitude: How do you feel about the situation and the receiver? Do you need to appear more confident, or examine your attitudes and prejudices towards the receiver?

Their attitude: Are they likely to be favourably disposed towards you, or are they likely to be prejudiced against you, or against the message? What previous knowledge might they have that you need to take into account?

Method of communication: Which means of communication is best suited to the situation, the receiver, the message? How should you pitch the message, and what type of language would be best to reach your intended receivers?

Now apply these principles to the following hypothetical cases:

● You want to contact somebody you met on holiday. You hope to meet him again and start a close friendship.

What do you need to consider and take into account regarding:

   – the situation
   – the content
   – the outcome
   – your attitude
   – his attitude.

What is your chosen method of communication, and why?

● You are working for an advertising agency. How would you sell a new sports car?

What do you need to consider and take into account regarding:

   – the situation
   – the content
   – the outcome

– your attitude

– the customers' attitude.

What is your chosen method of communication, and why?

• You want to complain to a manufacturer about a piece of string you found in a packet of frozen peas.

  What do you need to consider and take into account regarding:

  – the situation
  – the content
  – the outcome
  – your attitude
  – the manufacturer's attitude.

What is your chosen method of communication, and why?

Exercise 3: Receiving

As a receiver you're influenced by all the factors just discussed – if any are missing or misleading, you're not likely to give the response the sender is looking for. However, if you're on the receiving end, it's your responsibility to do two things: listen and understand. Difficulties in listening are likely to be caused by the following factors.

Feeling uncomfortable in a situation

Are you overawed by the person or situation? Are you unhappy with what is being said to you, or with what you think is expected from you? Are you too hot or too cold or choked by cigar smoke? It might help to remember that the person talking to you is likely to feel just as uncomfortable.

Being distracted

What was that noise? Is there something going on outside the window? What are you doing tonight? Have you ever seen hair quite that colour before? If you know you're easily distracted, try to keep yourself involved in what's being said. Consciously make an effort to respond or ask questions, or in situations like lectures, take notes.

Using inappropriate language

Is language inappropriate to the situation distracting you from the meaning? For instance, match the following situations:

1. 1930's play
2. building site
3. dog obedience class
4. office reception desk
5. Customs declaration form
6. job application form

with the appropriate language:

(a) Nom et addresse de l'expediteur.
(b) Would you like to sit down and wait?
(c) I say, old chap, would you mind passing one of those nice thingies?
(d) Name and address.
(e) Sit!
(f) Chuck us another one, Fred.

Using inappropriate language can totally distract the listener, and result in a totally unwanted response. For instance, if 2-c, 4-e, or 6-a are matched, the receiver is likely to be so put off by the language that s/he'll ignore the content of the message. The respective receivers are quite likely to 2. punch the sender in the nose, 4. report the receptionist's rudeness to her supervisor, or 6. decide not to apply, as they must be looking for someone who speaks French. Obviously, none of these is a result the sender wants.

Use of inappropriate body language

Imagine you're telling your boss about a great idea you've had to improve business. How would you interpret it if s/he:

- Yawned?
- Laughed?
- Looked out of the window?
- Took notes?
- Started to tap his/her fingers on the desk?
- Smiled and nodded?
- Frowned?
- Got up and walked away?
- Started talking to someone else while you were still talking?
- Leaned toward you?
- Put his/her arm around your shoulder?

When you are the listener, you need to be aware of your own reactions, and try to be aware of the effect of your actions upon the speaker.

Waiting for your turn to talk

Have you stopped listening because you're waiting to leap into a pause? Are you too busy thinking about your own response? Do you really care what the other person has to say? This situation can often be observed in television interviews, usually when the communicators are trying to impress each other or the audience. However, a clever communicator *will* listen to what is being said, and is likely to impress more, partly through being able to point out flaws in the other's argument.

Your attitude to a person or situation

Are you predisposed to co-operate (or resist) because you've taken an immediate like (or dislike) to the person? Are you going into the situation with a defensive attitude, because you feel strongly that the other person will be against you? If you have a negative attitude to the person or the situation, you're not likely to listen properly. This is a no-win situation.

The dreaded word 'bored' comes under this heading. 'Bored' is an attitude of mind. Anything and everything is boring if you are determined not to be interested or stimulated no matter what. If you are bored, you are inevitably boring.

Misunderstanding through incomplete messages

What does the following set of instructions describe? What information is missing? What's going to happen?

1. Plug in washing machine.
2. Switch on power at socket.
3. Put laundry into machine.
4. Put powder into machine.
5. Close door of machine.
6. Close powder drawer.
7. Set programme for washing.
8. Switch off machine.
9. Take out laundry.

Well, obviously, the instructions are for doing laundry. The missing information is to turn the machine on (and to put in coins, if you're at a launderette). And, therefore, nothing is going to happen.

Exercise 4: Apocryphal tale

You need complete information in order to respond intelligently. The following exercise illustrates that neatly. (Please don't read ahead – it'll spoil the punchline.)

1. You are working behind the counter in a shop. An elderly lady comes in carrying a bag, which she places on the counter. She looks worried.
   Answer the following questions: What is your impression of the lady? How do you feel towards her? Why do you think she might be worried? What might you say to her?

2. The little old lady rummages in the bag, pulls out a gun and points it at you.
   Answer the following questions: Have your feelings

towards her changed? Now how do you feel towards her? What might you say to her?

3. The lady tells you she found the gun outside in the street. She asks you what she should do with it.
   Answer the following questions: Now how do you feel towards her? What might you say to her? Would you trust her as much as when she first came into the shop?

Try to collect as many facts as possible before making a judgement.
A few tips to help you check your understanding:

- If you don't understand, ask. In almost every case, people will usually be pleased that you're showing an interest in what they're saying.
- You can say things like 'Do you mean . . . ?' and rephrase what's been said to you, to make sure you've got it right.
- Make notes on what you've been told or shown. You can then ask the other person to check that they're correct.
- Do not try to remember too many things at once. Write messages down and pass them on. This allows you to forget them if they're not for you.

Communication is all about understanding other people, and other people understanding you. To ensure good communication, you must be aware of *all* the messages you're sending to others and *all* the messages you're picking up from them.

Exercise 5: Communication analysis

This final exercise should be the culmination of all the work you've done so far on communication, assertiveness, transactions, and relationship building. If done carefully, in depth, and with considerable thought, it could have a marked effect on some aspects of your life.

Every day, we all find ourselves in a variety of situations where we have to communicate with different sorts of people. We are closely involved with some of them emotionally or circumstantially – husbands, parents, children, close friends. Some of them are in positions of authority over us – bank managers, bosses, DSS officers; some of them are simply part of our everyday operating environment – shop assistants, neighbours, milkmen, bus drivers .

We feel differently about all these people. We probably deal differently with all of them. And we probably could deal with some of them better.

Think about the various situations in your life where you communicate with others. Choose one that you'd like to improve. It might be within your family, a situation at work, your GP, or perhaps it concerns your children's school. Perhaps your choice will be suggested by columns you've marked with several 'X's' on the grid you completed in Chapter 8.

Now work through the following analysis. Take your time with it, really think it through. Ideally, you might want to recruit a partner to *talk* you through it, because explaining it to someone else will sharpen your own perceptions. (*Note*: If you decide to work with someone, make sure it's not a person directly involved with the situation you want to change.) Keep notes.

1. Briefly describe the situation you wish to analyse.
2. Who are the people involved in the situation? Describe them briefly.
3. What happens?
4. How often does it happen?
5. How long has it been happening?
6. Is the situation getting better or worse?
7. How do you feel about it?
8. How would you describe your ego state? Try to draw a picture or diagram of it.
9. What do you think is the ego state of the other(s) involved. Draw it.
10. What are you like to the other(s) in terms of:

   • respect
   • understanding
   • genuineness?

11. What are the other(s) like to you in terms of:

    - respect
    - understanding
    - genuineness?

12. Are you:

    submissive or assertive or aggressive?

13. Are the other(s):

    submissive or assertive or aggressive to you?

Take plenty of time thinking through your analysis, particularly if you're working on your own. You might want to sleep on it, and have another look at your notes over two or three days. Once you're satisfied that your analysis is a true representation of the situation, you're more than half way there.

Plan how you might deal differently at your next encounter. Keep a few notes on what you planned to do, what you expected the other(s) to do, and then make notes on what actually happened. Keep a particular eye out for use of body language: where the other(s) used body language to good effect; where you were able to judge the situation better or gauge your response based on your observation of their body language.

You should find that things improve. Even if you don't feel that you've successfully mastered all the techniques we've discussed, your communications will get better, simply because you're paying closer attention and because you have a bit more understanding of what's happening. But if at first you don't succeed, keep trying.

11

Action planning – 2

Back to the practicalities. We have spent the last few chapters primarily observing, thinking and analysing. We've turned our lives inside out, rearranged our psyches, examined our relationships and adjusted our interactions, and we are now facing the world from a brand-new perspective. Or something like that. Now we'll look at how the work has affected what we want and what we do.

Exercise 1: Goal setting

First take a look at your list of goals. When you're doing a course of aerobics, you can monitor your progress by stepping on a pair of scales and seeing how much weight you've lost. The measurable results give you a positive incentive to keep at it. If you want to compare where you were when you started with where you are now – to get a fairly good idea of the effectiveness of these exercises so far – this might be the right time for you to repeat the exercise on goal setting and prioritising.

Step 1

List all the things you want to achieve, all the things you want to do, and all the things you want to happen – now and in the future. Work quickly and include *everything* you can think of. Don't censor yourself, or leave anything out.

Step 2

Sort your list according to when you want to achieve each goal ('M' within the next month, 'Y' within the next year, or 'F' sometime in the future).

Step 3

Grade them according to their importance to you ('A' most important, 'B' less and 'C' least important).

Step 4

Delete all the B and C goals, regrading any that you decide you can't set aside at this time.

Step 5

Rank the A goals in order of importance (A1 most important and so forth).

Your new 'A' list is quite likely to look a bit different from the list you first compiled in Chapter 2. Compare your two goals lists, and then work through the following questions:

• Have you eliminated any of your original 'A' goals? Have you achieved any of them? Have you simply changed your mind about some of them? Why?
• Of those that are left, what have you accomplished so far?
• What goals are new to the list? Are some of them upgraded from your original 'B' and 'C' goals? Why? Are there any differences in the *kind* of goals you've added to your list?
• Have your priorities changed? In what way? Why? Make some brief notes on anything pertinent. You will then be able to refer to them later as you continue to gauge your progress.

You are next going to apply the Action Planning technique you tried out in Chapter 3 so that, if at all possible, you can get to work on *all* of your A goals this week. Do not be alarmed. It will be less complicated than you might think. You've taken on harder challenges before. An exercise like this is nothing compared to planning the average British family Christmas.

Christmas preparations can call for the logistical expertise of the Allied Command preparing to liberate France. It also takes a pool of creative talent equivalent to the production team on an average West End musical. Planning for Christmas requires knowledge about, skills in, and talent for: food, entertainment, transport, accommodation, relationships, memory, decorating, communications, timing, diplomacy . . . expand the list as you like, not forgetting finance. Entire books have been written on the subject of planning for Christmas.

If we can keep track of who eats what, who isn't speaking to whom, who gave whom what last year, who did and who didn't send a card, what our bank balance is vs when the bills are due, everybody's favourite colour . . . (and keep our heads when all about us are losing theirs), it *should* be obvious that we can handle just about anything. We deserve a medal. The only trouble is, when we look back on how much we've accomplished, we're more than likely to moan about how exhausting it all was, rather than taking pride in how well we did the job.

This brings us to action planning. Action planning, at the very least, makes it all less exhausting.

Exercise 2: Planning for action

Step 1

Using your list of 'A' goals, and starting with A1, draw up an action plan for each goal. Write your A1 goal at the top of a sheet of paper; then rule seven columns, as indicated in the chart overleaf.

GOAL: (*write in your goal*)

What has to be done	Priority A,B,C,D	Start when	Finish by	Who by	Resources needed	Completed

Step 2

Now think carefully about what needs to be done to accomplish this goal. Try to express these in terms of positive actions. Preferably these should be actions that you can control: either you're going to do it yourself, or you're able to supervise the person doing it in some way, or at least you're able to influence what happens. You might find it helpful to talk through the process with a friend before trying to write it down.

Try to keep your planned actions close to you in terms of responsibility. The further away they are, the less likely you are to have any influence. Try to keep the actions as close to the present as possible. The further away in time they are, the less likely they are to happen – you might change your mind or circumstances might change.

(If, for instance, you believe that to accomplish your goal you need to win the pools, the only part of that 'action' you have any control over is filling in your coupon and posting it. You'd be better off, in terms of action planning, to think of other ways to finance your goal. If, however, you think you need an Act of Parliament, you might make that a goal in itself, and start organising your campaign. This is likely to be a long-term effort. And, again, you might be better off trying to find alternative actions to accomplish your goal.)

Step 3

Following the chart, list each task separately, under 'what has to be done' and fill in the other columns as you go. (The 'completed' column will be ticked later when you accomplish the task.) For each action:

- decide on a specific timescale
- work out what resources you will need
- allocate responsibility for carrying out each action
- keep it realistic
- think about what support you will need.

Remember to work carefully, taking as much time as you need to think through each action completely. The more you are able to anticipate, the more likely you are to be able to control the results.

This principle, stated in its negative form, is called Murphy's Law: 'Anything that can go wrong, will go wrong' – with the corollary 'and at the worst possible time.' It is worth writing these words of wisdom in very large letters and very bright colours, and pinning them up where you cannot fail to see them. Particularly when planning for Christmas. *The more you are able to anticipate, the more likely you are to be able to control results.*

Step 4

When you have listed every action you can think of, prioritise them in terms of how urgent it is to get each done, and the importance of each in accomplishing your goal. Use the same system we used in Chapter 3: tasks which are Urgent and Important are Priority A, Urgent and Not Important are Priority B, not Urgent but Important are Priority C, and Not Urgent and Not Important are Priority D.

Step 5

Repeat the entire process for every goal on your A list.

You will find this technique for action planning easy and obvious for some of your goals, and relatively hard-going on others.

For instance, Judith's example A1 goal in Chapter 1 ('I want to be happy in what I do') could take some rather serious thinking.

If you have included that sort of goal on your list, it may not be easy at first to come up with positive, practical tasks which are within your own control, and which you can get started on immediately. But whether or not it's possible to achieve your goal in the near term, an honest attempt to express it in terms of positive personal action is likely to have a positive effect on your outlook/philosophy/approach to life.

Exercise 3: Seven-day plan

When you have completed action plans for all of your goals, it's a perfectly straightforward process to plan your next week. Simply check down your 'start when' column for dates in the seven days coming up, and highlight each one you find.

Start a new action plan sheet, headed 'Week of ____' (fill in Monday's date), and ruled with the same columns. Enter all the highlighted actions from all of the separate sheets. Then re-prioritise these actions, based on their relative importance and the practical considerations involved in doing them. That's your Seven-Day Action Plan. Keep it pinned above your desk, at the front of your diary, or wherever you're going to get the best use from it. Fill in the date you complete each task. If you find yourself falling behind schedule, make any adjustments needed to get back on course. Keep notes on:

- what went well;
- what went badly;
- what cropped up unexpectedly; and
- what changes you made

and review at the end of the week. Revise your lists of goals and actions as needed. Read Chapter 12. Then plan your actions for the next seven days.

12

Time management – 2

We've already demonstrated, through working on action plans and goal setting, that having a clear direction and setting sensible priorities are essential to good time management. But there are other practical techniques that can be used as well.

You may have found that putting your action plan into practice was less successful than it might have been, because you *ran out of time*, or *time slipped away* – somehow you just didn't have enough time to get everything done. Time can seem to be almost supernatural – it's abstract, intangible, elusive. You can't pin it down. It *flies*.

Forget all that. Time is a valuable resource. In business terms, time is a commodity which is calculated in man-hours. It must be paid for, it must be allocated economically, and at the end of the day it must be accounted for. Time used must be justified. Lost time must be made up. Time is studied – highly paid consultants try to determine where and how time can be saved. In the business world, time really is money. It is spent. It can also be wasted or stolen.

Exercise 1: A waste of time

Work through the following hypothetical case:

The WP Bureau is a word processing service, which is a full-time one-woman operation run by Ms Wanda Price. Wanda charges her customers £1 per page. Her average typing speed is fifty words per minute, which means it takes her about five minutes to type one page.

5 minutes per page = 12 pages per hour
12 × 7 working hours = 84 pages per day
84 × 5 days = 420 pages per week
420 × 52 weeks = 21,840 pages per year
21,840 pages = £21,840 gross income per year

True or false: Wanda's word processing bureau produces a gross income of £21,840 per year.

Answer: False, for what should be obvious reasons. Wanda's *productive* time must be far less than her total time at the office. In fact, her turnover is only about £10,000. Can you list at least eight to ten reasons why?

Some of the answers are easy. Others may surprise you. Check yours against the following.

1. She takes four weeks holiday a year.
2. The bureau is closed on ten Public Holidays a year.
*3. She was ill for five working days.
4. She had three days unpaid leave (responsibilities towards her children).
5. She had two mornings off to go to the dentist.
*6. A snowstorm cut off the electricity for a day.
*7. The computer was down for three days.
*8. All the work done on the day before the computer went down was lost and had to be redone.
*9. Tea breaks, going to the toilet, chatting and so forth takes 10 per cent of every day (the national average).
*10. Computer maintenance, cleaning up files, and so forth takes about 10 per cent of the day.
*11. Answering the phone and dealing with visitors takes up 10 per cent of the day.
*12. One job in forty has to be completely redone.
*13. Following a mixup over re-ordering, she ran out of cartridges for the printer and it took four days for delivery.

*14. Setting up each job, formatting and printing adds an average of two minutes per page.

Although there's not a lot Wanda can do about some of the items listed, those marked * would allow room for improvement.

Exercise 2: Keeping time

Step 1

Gather some evidence. Repeat the time keeping exercise (Chapter 1) for one day. Keep an accurate diary of your time use, this time paying particular attention to unproductive time.

For example, if Wanda were doing this exercise, she might as a matter of course log how long she spends on each separate typing job – but for the purposes of this exercise, she should also log how many minutes she spends away from the keyboard each time she answers the phone, or takes a tea break, loses time through mistakes, chats to friends and so forth.

We'll define *unproductive* time simply as time when you should have been getting something else done, or getting it done faster. (*Note*: Constructive leisure time is *not* unproductive time – it's good for you. We all need to allow ourselves time to unwind.)

Step 2

When you've built up a good picture of where your time goes, work through the diary with a coloured pen and mark the unproductive time which you've *wasted*.

Wasted time is unproductive time that's largely under your own control. Examples might be:

• watching television for a full half-hour, rather than the five-minute weather forecast you meant to catch

- reading through a junk mail catalogue, rather than tossing it straight into the bin
- spending forty minutes searching through your unsorted box of recipes, and then cooking the chicken the same way as always
- trying on three different outfits before deciding what you're going to wear to the party.

Step 3

Add it all up. Then list as many things as you can think of that you could have done with that time if you hadn't wasted it.

Step 4

Divide a sheet of paper into two vertical columns. In the left column, list all the different ways you waste time. Use as many sheets as you need – you want to put down every possible thing you can think of. Take a good long time to think it through – there may be considerably more time-wasters than turned up in the one day you monitored.

When you've finished your list, think about what you can do to minimise the time you waste – or, even better, to prevent yourself wasting that time in the first place. You'll need to call on your planning and prioritising skills, and probably a bit of self-discipline. Use the right-hand column to 'answer' each time-waster you've listed.

Step 5

Finally, take a large piece of paper and a brightly coloured felt tip pen. Write the following in big letters:

IF YOU WASTE YOUR TIME
YOU'RE WASTING YOUR LIFE

Post it in a prominent position, so that it's clearly visible from the place where you waste the most time.

Exercise 3: The time pirates

Step 1

Work through the following hypothetical case.

Helen is a Home Help. She thinks that most of the old people she visits are really nice. For some of them, having someone to talk to is very important. They are on their own most days, and when Helen comes round they want to talk, and talk, and talk. She tries to listen, but she has to get on with work she's required to do during the visit as well. She could easily end up chatting all day if she weren't careful.

Helen has other people to visit – four a day in total – and has a family of her own to see to as well. If she gets behind, she'll have to either spend a shorter time with some, or put in extra time (unpaid). The latter would mean Helen will get home late.

- What is Helen's problem?
- How can she do both parts of the job – getting the work done, as well as talking and listening to people?

Step 2

Take another look at your diary of unproductive time. Using a different coloured pen, mark the time that's been stolen from you. We'll define *stolen* time as time that's unproductive because of circumstances which are largely beyond your control, generally because of the actions of other people. Examples might be:

- having to wait at the airport for several hours because European flight controllers are working to rule;
- spending your entire day dealing with your best friend's sudden romantic crisis;
- having to set your own work aside when your boss interrupts with his priority (but you'll still be required to meet the deadline on your own work); or
- spending your entire day waiting for the repairman to show up (they don't make specific appointments).

Step 3

When you've marked all the time that has been stolen from you in one day, make a list of all the things you might have done with that time.

Step 4

Next, make a list (two columns) of all your Time Pirates – the people who steal your time. In the left column, write the name of each one, and after each complete this sentence: 'S/he steals my time by . . .'

Whilst in many cases you won't be able to prevent people from stealing your time, you can usually do something to rescue some of it. Think about what you could do to prevent your time being stolen, or to rescue some of the time that's been taken. (Take your time.)

Step 5

In the right-hand column, write all the ideas you come up with against each example of piracy. In some cases, all you can do is anticipate and, for instance, bring your knitting to the airport so the time is put to some constructive use. In situations like 'your best friend's crisis', you'll need to weigh the priorities of your own needs against those of your Pirate friend, and use all the communication/relationship/transaction skills at your command to deal with her.

Exercise 4: Time management practice

From your lists, select one example each of wasted and stolen time that you'd like to work on. Over the next few days, try to put into practice some of your ideas for dealing with them. Keep brief notes on how well you succeed. For a really tight comparison, you might want to keep a time diary again, add up time wasted and time stolen, and then check it against your first efforts to monitor progress. Keep trying until you see some real improvement.

Exercise 5: Action plan

Go back to Chapter 11 and repeat the seven-day plan, this time taking care to avoid wasted or stolen time.

One last thought: you don't get a second chance to use a piece of time – once it's gone, it's gone for good.

13

The course of your life

In this chapter you're going to produce a short autobiography called 'The Course of My Life'. As any celebrity who has just published her memoirs is likely to say to the chat show host, putting your life story down on paper is worth *years* of therapy sessions. You might question the truth of that statement – and certainly nobody means to imply that anyone reading this book *needs* therapy. But we've already demonstrated that putting events and relationships into perspective on paper – even just putting them into sequence – can be a real eye-opener. Most important, it can have a positive effect on how you feel about yourself.

Celebrities write their autobiographies because a publisher believes thousands of people will want to read it. It also gives them something new to say on chat shows. You may not be a celebrity, you may never appear on a chat show, but dozens (perhaps even hundreds) of people in the course of your life will want to read the story of *your* life.

You may, however, want to change the title – 'The Course of My Life' might not appeal to everyone. If you prefer (and almost everybody does), you can translate it into Latin, which is *Curriculum Vitae* – CV for short.

Compiling a CV is a useful exercise for anyone. You don't necessarily have to be looking for a job, working towards a promotion, applying for a bank loan, or using it in any other business context. Putting together an orderly record of what you've accomplished so far in the course of your life can be a bit like spring cleaning – a chance for a general sort-out.

Exercise 1:   Preparing your CV

A Master CV is the complete record of everything you've done since the year dot. This version will be For Your Eyes Only – you aren't likely to send it unedited to a prospective employer or anyone else. Rather, the Master CV is your own permanent resource document, from which you'll later be able to select appropriate information for a variety of specific purposes. Nevertheless, to make it easier to adapt for future uses, you'll want to follow a standard CV format.

There are any number of styles and formats you can use for a Curriculum Vitae. Your choice will depend mainly on clarity and convenience – how comfortably does your information fit into it? Most CVs are arranged in columns and contain approximately the same information, although not necessarily in the same order. (The example in Fig. 13.1 is typical.)

Using the example as a model, compile your own Master CV. Take your time, be thorough – you might want to work on this over the course of several days, and add to the CV as you remember more things. It will be time and effort well spent. The more detailed and comprehensive you make it, the more useful the document will be to you in future.

You might find it helpful to refer to some of the work you did earlier on skills identification and roles played, to jog your memory and help you build up a complete picture of each job, activity and accomplishment in your life. Keep your timescales in perspective, though – your achievements in secondary school, for instance, will take on more importance and be described in more detail if you're twenty-ish, than they will be if you're forty-something!

Remember: you are creating this document for your own benefit, so you don't need to censor or edit out *any* of your background. That said, it's important to state everything in simple, straightforward, *positive* terms: just write down what

Curriculum Vitae

Mary Christine JONES

365 East Orchard Street
Bridgwater, Somerset TA25 7YY
Telephone: (0278) 666555

Education:	Northdown Sixth Form College – 1972–74		
	Northdown Comprehensive School – 1968–72		

Other training:	Bridgwater College, Adult Education
	Wordprocessing & computer course – 1987

Examinations:	1974 – RSA Typing and Office Skills		
	1973 – O-level	English language	Grade B
		Needlework	Grade B
		Ancient History	Grade A
	CSE	French	Grade 2
		Mathematics	Grade 1
		Metalwork	Grade 3

Experience

1988-Present	Selfbury's, Taunton – Computer Clerk
	Responsibilities: Database work (input, amendment and retrieval on DBase III); word processing (Word Perfect, text and statistical).
1980-1988	Voluntary work, part-time, including:
	Oxfam, shop assistant
	St Johns Ambulance, fundraising activities
	Milbrook Primary School, classroom assistant
1974-1980	Grabbit Property Services, Taunton – Secretary
	Responsibilities: Typing (60 wpm), shorthand (110 wpm), filing; preparation of property leaflets and adverts; fielding enquiries from public; deputising for property negotiators as needed.

Other skills:	Full, clean driving licence; fluent French
Personal data:	Date of Birth: 11 January 1957
	Married, 2 children
Interests:	Secretary, Running Mead Carnival Club; horse riding; reading; listening to music

Referees:	Mrs R Smith	Mr L Clark
	Office Manager	Manager
	Selfbury's Ltd	Grabbit Property Services
	Selfbury House	Eastgate
	Exeter Road	Wiveliscombe
	Taunton	Taunton, Somerset TA4 6NN
	Somerset TA1 7JJ	(0823) 555444
	(0823) 444555	

you did and when, with minimal explanation and absolutely no apologies!

1. Write 'Curriculum Vitae' at the top (usually centred). [*Options*: it can go after your name, address and phone number; *or* you can omit it completely, because any-body can see at a glance that it's a CV, and it wastes a whole line to tell them so.]

2. Put your name, address and phone number, in block formation, either at the left margin or centred. If possible, emphasise your name (for example, by using bold type). In any case, your surname should be in capital letters. Be sure to include your full post code with the address, and national STD code with the telephone number.

The following information should be set out as clearly as possible, so that anyone reading it can glance down and pick out the particular things that interest them without effort. Usually these items are arranged in columns, with headings down the left:

3. *Education*: List schools attended and dates. Include such things as Open University courses, even if you're still working on them.

4. *Examinations (and other academic qualifications)*: A-levels, O-levels, RSA, City & Guilds, University degrees and any other such qualifications here, specifying the subjects covered in each. [*Option*: Some people rec-ommend including grades obtained, even for those subjects you didn't pass. Others would advise you to include grades only if they're particularly impressive, and to list subjects not passed as 'other subjects studied' if at all. For a Master CV, include everything.]

Professional qualifications or affiliations: If you belong to the Plumbers' Guild, Actors' Equity, or the Society of Doing Whatever, include them here under 'Professional Affiliations'. If you've had to pass an exam or be passed by an examining board to have letters after your name (if you're a qualified chartered accountant, for instance), that should be included separately, under 'Professional Qualifications'.

5. *Other training*: Any relevant non-exam courses, workshops, seminars, or training. [*Option*: Less relevant courses can be included below, under 'Interests'.]

6. *Experience*: All of your work experience, in date order, starting with the most recent. Put the dates you worked in the left-hand column. [*Option*: Stating just the years (ie, 1989–1991) is generally sufficient, although some people prefer to use the month or the full date.] Each entry should clearly indicate:
   – the employer's name and location (although not the full address);
   – your job title(s), including any history of promotion, especially where you had different kinds of experience within the same company; [*Option*: List only the highest level you achieved in the job];
   – what you actually did in the particular job. Don't forget all the work you did on skills, time use, and roles. For the purposes of a master CV, you want to list absolutely every different thing you did in each job, including specialist knowledge, such as specific computer programmes or filing systems you might have used. (You may edit it later as needed.) [*Option*: Voluntary work may be listed as a separate major heading, with or without dates. It is important, however, to try to avoid holes in your work history, so it might be useful to include such activities within the chronological list of jobs, as in the example.]

7. *Other skills*: Literally, anything else you know how to do that might come in handy on a job. [*Option*: You could call this section 'Miscellaneous.']

8. *Personal data*: Such information as date of birth, marital status, number and age of children, nationality, and so forth, are usually included here. However, *ALL of this is optional*. If asked (for instance, on an applica-

tion form), you must of course tell the truth, but you don't have to volunteer any of this information on your CV if you don't want to.

9. *Interests*: Hobbies, pastimes, activities to make you look like a well-rounded individual, and to give the interviewer something non-business to chat about. (More about which in subsequent chapters.) Again, tell the truth, and – since this is the master document – list everything you can think of. You will edit it down to a sensible length later.

10. *Referees*: Usually an employer will want two referees, but for the purposes of a master CV, you'll want a choice of perhaps four – two of them work-related (including your current employer or a recent one) and two of them personal. Never include anyone who is related to you. Always ask permission before you list anyone as a referee, and wherever possible, brief them on the requirements of the job and suggest what you'd like them to vouch for. [*Options*: When sending out a CV, many people prefer not to list referees unless they're specifically asked for. The employer generally will state how many to include (two is standard), and whether personal or professional referees are wanted. Alternatively, you can choose to name your referees in a cover letter, or simply state 'references on request' at the bottom of the CV if the employer hasn't specified that they're wanted.]

When you're reasonably satisfied that your master CV is complete in every detail, make a clean copy (preferably typed) to keep for future reference. If you have access to a word processor, store your complete master CV on disc, so that you can edit and amend it as needed later.

In Chapter 15 we will look at how to slant a CV to fit a particular job or situation. But, first a bit of theory and practice on the art of selling.

111

14

Selling

Everyone has to sell something sometime. You may never work in a dress shop or telesales office, you may never trudge from door to door trying to convince people to buy double-glazing – but there will often be times in your life when you have to give someone a sales pitch. We all find ourselves in 'selling' situations daily. Our 'customers' can be family, friends, co-workers, bank managers – or just about anyone we deal with.

We may sell our houses to prospective buyers. We may sell raffle tickets and poppies for charity. We may 'sell' a holiday package to a husband or partner or flatmate – and our sales pitch in this case might have to be better than the travel agent's. There is no doubt whatsoever that it takes saleswomanship of a high order to be successful in 'selling' muesli for breakfast to our children, instead of choco-sugar krunchies with cartoons on the box.

In business and professional contexts, in addition to selling actual products to actual customers, we may also have to 'sell' our suggestions to a superior, or our ideas to a client. Or we may 'sell' our skills and services to a prospective employer, or a business idea to a bank manager.

Exercise 1: Selling situations

Step 1

As a warm-up, try to think of a recent situation when you succeeded in selling something – perhaps in a situation similar to any of the examples given above. Bearing in mind the work we've done previously on communication in all its various aspects, work through the following questions. Make brief notes as you go.

- Describe the situation. What did you want to sell, and to whom?
- Was it important? To you? To your 'customer'? Why?
- How did you feel about making your sales pitch? Did you find it easy or difficult? Do you know why?
- Think through the points you made about your product or idea, and how your customer responded to each. Can you draw any conclusions about why you were successful? If so, list them.

Step 2

For comparison purposes, think of another recent selling situation – this time one when you were less successful. Again, work through the following, making brief notes.

- Describe the situation. What did you want to sell, and to whom?
- Was it important? Why? Do you think it was less important to you than your previous example? Was it more or less important to your customer?
- How did you feel in this situation about making your sales pitch? Did you find it more difficult? Why?
- Again, think through the points you made about your product or idea, and how your customer responded to each. Can you see any basic differences between this time and your successful example? If so, make a note of them.

Saleswomanship

Whilst it may be true that some people are 'born salesmen' (or women), there is no question that sales techniques can be learned, and can be improved with practice. The sales process – whether in a shop, on the phone, in advertising, or translated into situations within your job or your family – consists of seven main stages:

1. Greet the customer and find out his or her needs
2. Present and demonstrate features of the product or service
3. Identify the benefits
4. Deal with queries and objections
5. Close the sale
6. Make alternative or additional sales
7. Provide after sales service.

Exercise 2: The sales process

Apply the seven-stage sales process to the two selling situations you described in Exercise 1. Try to fit what happened into the seven-part model. Be sure to cover your approach, your *customer's* response, and any follow-on. (This may not be easy, but the process will make sense to you if you take the time to write it out.) When you've taken it as far as you can, consider whether any of the seven points were missing from your sales pitch. Where is there room for improvement?

The following discussion points might help to clarify the process for you. Stages 1, 4 and 7 are at the heart of customer relations. You can think of customer relations in terms of a specialist application of the work we did in the chapters on communication, relationships, transactions and (for some) assertiveness.

Listening for queries and objections raised by the customer is particularly important. Don't dismiss them or try to override them. A question or objection can often be a 'buying signal' – an indication that the customer is close to the point of buying. Some examples are:

- The customer raises a genuine objection.
- The customer asks you for more information.
- The customer asks you to go over the details again.
- The customer makes a 'committing statement' (for instance, 'If I could spread the payments I might be interested').
- The customer brings in a friend or partner for a second opinion.

Each of these buying signals could allow you to repeat the features and benefits. As we'll demonstrate next, that is an advantage. Just remember to be patient and stay interested.
[*Note*: Queries and objections might also be a sign that you're presenting the wrong product (even if you've been trying to sell them what they *said* they wanted). Try to find out what they really need, and supply that if you can. This comes under Stage 6 in the model, *Alternative Sales*.]

Benefit selling

Stages 2 and 3, *Features* and *Benefits* are the key points on which a discerning customer will make a decision. Identifying the *features* of a product or service, and then being able to demonstrate them clearly, should be a fairly straightforward exercise:

- What is it made of?
- How is it made?
- What does it do?
- How much does it cost?
- What quality is it?
- Who manufactures it?
- How is it different from the competitors?
- What size, colour, duration? . . . and so forth

On the other hand, identifying, and then selling, the *benefits* may take some practice. Benefit selling is as much a way of thinking as it is a sales technique. Instead of selling *things* to customers, you sell the *advantages that owning the things will bring to the customer*.

The customer may have asked for a specific product or service – but it's your job, as a salesperson, to ask why. Is the customer *really* looking for 'pay-offs' such as status, efficiency, popularity, or freedom from worry? Buying the product or service is simply the customer's way of getting the pay-off. Pay-offs are benefits.

In order to 'sell the benefits', you need to think in terms of each feature leading to one or more benefits. If, for instance, you are trying to sell a video recorder:

- *Don't* sell an electronic device to record TV programmes or watch pre-recorded films.

- *Do* sell cheap family entertainment, freedom to watch favourite programmes when you choose, and a means to avoid family arguments when programmes clash.

Exercise 3: Working out the benefits

Step 1

For each item listed below, identify the main features and then the benefits attached to each feature:

a deodorant; a weekend break in London; a pension; a fitness club; a car; a dishwasher; a home cleanser; and a mail order catalogue service.

Step 2

Advertising relies heavily on the technique of benefit selling. For practice, over the next few days, analyse advertisements that you see on television or read in newspapers and magazines. Keep notes on the products (or services or ideas) being sold, on the features demonstrated, the benefits identified, and most particularly, on where the emphasis has been placed.

Exercise 4: Sales promotion

Sales technique boils down to a few simple principles:

- *Grab the attention*. Before you can communicate the benefits, you have to get the audience to look at you or listen to what you have to say. You can make the benefits stand out from the rest by using key words, colour, and visual images.
- *Keep it short and simple*. Keep the message clear and straightforward. Don't use too many words, jargon, or long involved sentences.
- *Sell the benefits*. Make sure the benefits are stated early on in the sales communication.
- *Make it appropriate*. Many sales pitches come across as 'over the top' or insincere because the person communicating has forgotten to consider and make allowances for the expectations of the audience. Think about who you are communicating to, how they would expect something to be presented, and what images they associate with the items being sold.

As a final exercise, pick any specific item and create a piece of advertising material for it. This might be a brochure, a poster or a magazine advert. Your promo piece should cover all four of the points listed above.

In the next chapter, we're going to apply the selling techniques we've practised in a more specialised application.

15

Selling yourself

Let there be no misunderstanding about the title of this chapter. 'Selling yourself' means *positive personal promotion*: using the sales techniques we looked at in Chapter 14 – and most particularly benefit selling – as they apply to your own experience and abilities.

This exercise shouldn't be new to you. There are any number of day-to-day situations when we all want to present ourselves in the best possible light. These are often social situations – tea with the vicar, meeting new people of any sort, or perhaps a dinner when we particularly want to impress the guests. We're on our best behaviour, clean the house especially carefully, cook special recipes, wear our most becoming clothes, and watch what we say.

In these situations, we automatically try to edit out the less impressive features of our lives in order to create a good impression. And there are occasionally times when we try to *put a good face on* negative circumstances, which might be anything from disappointing to disastrous.

Similar situations happen in business: taking a client to lunch, rehearsing a presentation, tidying up the office for a VIP visit, dressing up for an important meeting, planning in advance what to say – and most especially what not to say! And, needless to say, promotional literature, advertising and publicity all are designed to put a good face on everything – they emphasise *only* the good side of the story.

Arguably the most common – and the most critical – situation where an individual needs to create a good impression is when applying for a job. To practise our selling technique, we are going to work through the techniques of benefit selling in the specific context of demonstrating to an employer the advantages to be gained in hiring you.

Please note that, even if you're not currently jobhunting, this exercise is well worth the time and effort you'll spend. Its underlying benefit to you should be to reinforce all the work we've done so far in self-awareness and self-confidence. And, in any case, the techniques we'll practise adapt equally well to other situations in life where you might be 'under consideration': moving up the ladder in your present job, getting a bank loan to finance your business idea, being accepted at a university, running for office in an organisation, and possibly even (but this applies only to heroines of romance novels) getting your man to propose!

Exercise 1: Situations Vacant

Step 1

Find an appropriate job to practise the technique. Read through the Situations Vacant section of the newspaper of your choice. Either local or national papers will do, so long as there are plenty of suitable jobs to look at. As this is a practice session, you don't need to be concerned about such things as location, salary, possible competition for the position advertised, or whether you would have a snowball's chance to get it if you actually applied. You want to choose an advert to work on, based on the following criteria only:

- the content of the job must be described fairly fully;
- the skills and qualities required of candidates must be specified;
- based on the description given, the job must really appeal to you; and
- regardless of whether you think you could get such a job, you *must* believe that you are capable of doing it.

Step 2

When you have found a suitable example, work through the following questions, making brief notes as you go:

1. What does the advert tell you about your customer (ie, the employer)?
2. What are the customer's needs?
3. What *features* is the customer looking for in the product (ie, the candidate)?
4. Can you pick out any *key words* from the ad copy?
5. What aspects of your experience most closely fit the requirements?
6. List anything you've done in the past that is similar to the job described. Why are they similar? Be specific.
7. What about the job appeals to you most, and why?
8. Do you have any doubts about the job? List them.
9. Can you anticipate any doubts the employer might have about you? List them – and then answer them, positively.
10. What makes you think you can do this job?
11. What are the *benefits* to the employer in hiring you?

The example opposite was drawn from a local paper in the Southwest: You might be able to extract the following information from it.

About the company: It's a big company and concerned about its image (the advert was large and well-designed). It is proud of its product. It values its customers. It also values its sales negotiators ('instrumental' and good rate of pay). It has a training programme. The Sales Director is a woman.
About the job: You might be working on your own. The job requires training. You'll be dealing with people. You'll be able to move up quickly, based on merit. You'll have to work on weekends. There is probably administrative work involved ('organised') and it will probably be done manually ('in your own handwriting') rather than on computer. Some of the salary will be commission.

SALES NEGOTIATOR

If you think that the following description fits you, you could be the person we're looking for:

You're aged between 30 and 45, self-motivated and a good organiser. You enjoy meeting people from all backgrounds and are able to converse clearly with them. You have a smart appearance and can work on your own initiative.

As a Homesweet Homes Sales Negotiator, you'll be instrumental in the sale of new Homesweet Homes, and your enthusiasm for the job will help make buying a new home easy for our purchasers.

Full training will be given, and you'll be responsible for your own site as soon as you've proven your ability.

Good basic pay plus a commission package will give you a potential salary of up to £13,000 p.a.

You'll receive 4 weeks holiday and work a 5 day week, 11 am – 6 pm, including Saturdays and Sundays.

Applications are invited in your own handwriting, to: **Mrs Jane Smith, Sales Director, Homesweet Homes Ltd, High Street, Bristol BS1 4XX.**

What is required from the candidate: Maturity. Communication and 'people' skills. Self-confidence. Self-motivation, enthusiasm. Outgoing personality. Good appearance. Good handwriting (or they might possibly employ a graphologist to analyse the applications).
Key words: Self-motivated. Organiser. Enjoy. All backgrounds. Converse clearly. Smart. Initiative. Instrumental. Enthusiasm. Responsible. Ability.

Exercise 2: Slanting the CV

Your next step will be to create a CV that is suitable for the job you've selected. It might be helpful to think of your CV as a piece of promotional literature that you will send out to prospective customers. In other words, it is like a direct mail advertisement for yourself. It must fulfil the requirements of any sales material: it should *grab the attention*, be *short and simple*, *sell the benefits*, and be *appropriate to the audience*.

If you have put enough thought into compiling a thorough master CV, it should be a simple matter to edit it. Your finished CV should fit on one page, if possible, and it must emphasise those parts of your experience which most closely match the job description in the ad you've chosen. The following will give you an idea of how you might do it.

If Mary Christine Jones (our sample CV in Chapter 13) were applying for the Sales Negotiator job described above, she would want to emphasise the *administrative* aspects of her present computer clerk job, as well as areas where she's shown initiative and responsibility. She might stress her *contact with people* and organising ability in the voluntary work. And, most particularly, she should be sure to point out the many similarities between working in an estate agent's office and selling new houses.

Therefore, her estate agency job, which on her master CV reads:

Grabbit Property Services, Taunton – Secretary
Responsibilities: Typing (60 wpm), shorthand (110 wpm), filing; preparation of property leaflets and adverts; fielding enquiries from the public; deputising for the property negotiators as needed.

might now be edited to read:

Grabbit Property Services, Taunton – Secretary
Responsibilities: deputising for property negotiators, often having full charge of the office; discussing customers' needs and providing them with information

on properties (including newly-built homes); arranging for them to view properties (accompanying them if needed); liaison with people selling their homes; preparation of property leaflets and adverts; secretarial and administrative duties.

Note that, even though she may have spent most of her time on secretarial duties, these are listed only briefly and last, because they are least relevant to this particular application. Such details as typing and shorthand speed are omitted.

Dealing with doubts

What if, for instance, Mary were 28 or 47 years of age? The ad specified 30-45 – should she bother to apply? There's not a lot you can do about the occasional under-briefed but over-zealous personnel assistant who sorts applications according to the letter of the law. In most cases, however, such a specification is not strictly a question of age. The employer is trying to convey an impression of the sort of person they're looking for. Often this is simply the sort of person they've hired previously. What the employer is really saying in this case, is that they want someone who is mature, but who couldn't be described as middle-aged. So they should be perfectly happy with someone who is demonstrably mature and responsible at 25, or youthful and energetic at 50.

What can you do to get around it? We have already established that whatever you do, you don't lie! On an application form, you'd have to fill in the dates honestly where they were specifically asked for. You should then be sure to demonstrate that you're otherwise a strong enough candidate so that your age won't matter.

Since this is a CV, all Mary would need to do is omit her date of birth, and perhaps her school dates as well. If her CV demonstrates that she is suitable in other ways, the omission of dates may not even be noticed. If the employer is really keen to pinpoint her age, it can be worked out approximately (although not necessarily accurately) from her employment dates, which she should still include. And again, if asked at the interview, she should tell

123

the truth. (If it counted against her at this point, she might not be happy at that job anyhow.) More about interviews in the next chapter.

Remember: Nobody's perfect. Employers hope, but don't really expect to find the absolutely perfect candidate for every job. You may have doubts about the strength of your CV, but it's important to remember never to volunteer an apology or explanation about a supposed weakness – that will only call attention to it. Good sales strategy must always be to stress the positive points.

Wherever possible, you want to transform possible weaknesses in your CV into positive points. For instance, if you've worked at a variety of different jobs, all of them for short periods, you can point to your versatility and breadth of experience. You might also note the common thread among them (they all involved dealing with people, and so forth) to indicate your underlying consistency.

If you don't have the specific qualification that's asked for, describe your relevant experience and knowledge *at length*. Remember, in many cases the qualification will be 'preferred' or 'helpful' rather than required. You may be able to get the qualification *after* you've got the job. Indicating your interest in studying for the qualification might earn you points for enthusiasm.

On the other hand, if you have the qualification, but not the experience, then emphasise the qualification, and talk about the content of the coursework you did to earn it.

Exercise 3: Cover letters

You may have noted that our example Situations Vacant ad did not ask for a CV. You would have the option, in this case, to write a good letter of application containing the relevant information (which will, again, be drawn from your master CV). Wherever possible, such a letter should be limited to a single, uncrowded page. This can often work to your advantage, because you have the opportunity to point out those *features* about yourself and *benefits* to the employer which are most *relevant* to the particular job, but there won't be room to include the rest.

If it's not possible to fit all the information you want to include on one page, send a CV – even if it hasn't been specified – with a short cover letter. The letter will, again, *sell the benefits*, as well as identify the most relevant *features* that you want the employer to look for in the enclosed CV.

Both in letters of application and in cover letters, it can be a good idea to use the *key words* you've extracted from the job description wherever you can, without being obvious. This is a subtle technique to build up an impression in the employer's mind that the person who wrote the letter seems to fit the requirements. Key words drawn from our sales negotiator ad are in italics in the following example:

> 'My experience with Grabbit Property Services is per-haps most relevant. I was *responsible* for *organis-ing* . . . On those occasions when I was *in sole charge* of the office, I particularly *enjoyed helping our clients* select from our *wide range* of properties . . .'

When you are satisfied that your CV plus cover letter (or your letter of application) communicate clearly that you are a person who is able to do the job and well worth hiring, type them. (If the ad you've chosen specifies 'in your own handwriting', the letter should, of course, be handwritten. A CV should always be typed.)

Pointers on Presentation

Neatness counts. Spelling counts. Use good quality, plain paper. Coloured paper might help *grab attention* – but limit your choice to cream, ivory, or possibly pale gray. You might consider straying into pastels or even something livelier – but only if you're absolutely sure it would be *appropriate* for the company *and the position* you're applying for. (For example, a children's theatre company, a trendy boutique, or a new age restaurant might welcome an application that's mildly eccentric – but not

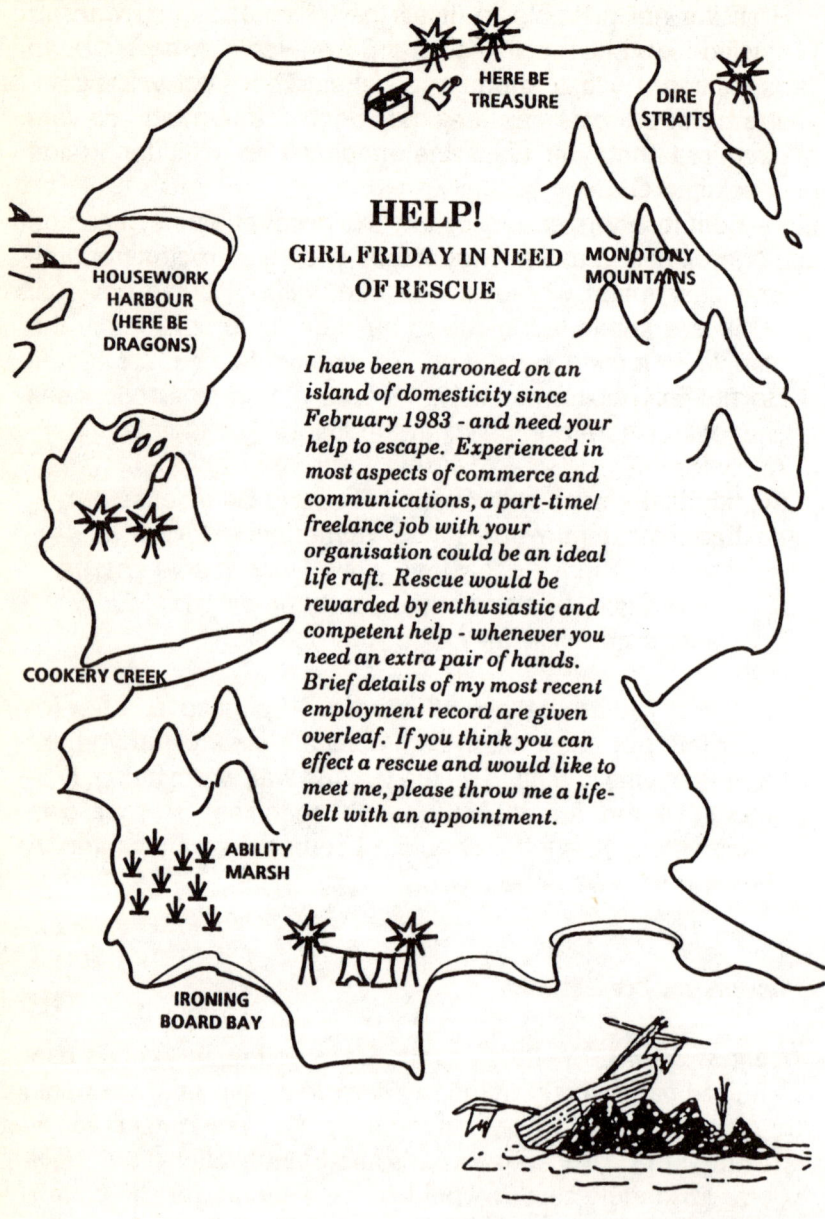

The following text labels appear on the map illustration:

HERE BE TREASURE

DIRE STRAITS

HOUSEWORK HARBOUR (HERE BE DRAGONS)

MONOTONY MOUNTAINS

HELP!

GIRL FRIDAY IN NEED OF RESCUE

I have been marooned on an island of domesticity since February 1983 - and need your help to escape. Experienced in most aspects of commerce and communications, a part-time/ freelance job with your organisation could be an ideal life raft. Rescue would be rewarded by enthusiastic and competent help - whenever you need an extra pair of hands. Brief details of my most recent employment record are given overleaf. If you think you can effect a rescue and would like to meet me, please throw me a life-belt with an appointment.

COOKERY CREEK

ABILITY MARSH

IRONING BOARD BAY

THE WRECK OF "THE INDEPENDENT LADY"

Figure 15.1 An innovative cover letter

necessarily from a bookkeeper.) *Be careful*! If there is even a shadow of doubt, always make the conservative choice.

However, it must be said that if you're trawling for interest in you as an individual, rather than applying for a specific job, you can't rule out using an innovative approach – particularly if you're trying to find something out of the ordinary. The Treasure Map cover letter (Fig. 15.1) generated by a participant on one of our earlier courses actually netted her 50 per cent results – admittedly from places like children's theatre companies and New Age boutiques. She ultimately got a job at a health food shop.

Bonus Exercise

Apply for the job. Send in your CV and/or letter. If you make the shortlist – very well done indeed. You'll want to read the next chapter before you go to the interview.

16

Interviews

To most people, the thought of going for an interview is something like going to the dentist – a necessary ordeal which they'd prefer to do as seldom as possible. This is especially true for job interviews. Just as constructing your CV was an advanced exercise in written communication (plus selling), learning to cope successfully at a job interview can be considered a sort of final exam in advanced verbal and visual communication (plus selling).

It may help to relieve any anxiety you might have about interviews to consider the following: people who are used to interview situations – notably journalists, chat show hosts, and various kinds of celebrities – firmly believe that being interviewed is far easier than having to ask the questions themselves. Unlike a trip to the dentist, they'd rather be on the receiving end.

Interviews are a two-way communication. The person sitting behind the desk may be more nervous about it than you are. How does this help you? What can you do with the information? You can do what you can to make the interview easy for the interviewer. Be reassuring. Play 'I'm OK – You're OK'.

Exercise 1: I'm OK

There are a number of things you can do to make sure that you *are*, in fact, OK.

Step 1

Plan ahead. These are some of the basics that you can sort out well in advance:

Logistics
Where is the interview? How will you get there? How long will it take you to get there? Make sure your transport is *absolutely* reliable. Make sure that, no matter what, you're able to get there on time – and preferably early. As an exercise, you might check out maps, routes and public transport schedules in your area and so forth, to plan how you'd get to an interview for the job you 'applied for' in Chapter 15.

Appearance
What are you going to wear? This is not a frivolous question. This is visual communication. You need to be dressed appropriately. Better than that, you want to make your clothes work for you. An actor being interviewed for a part would dress the way that character might dress. A celebrity being interviewed on a chat show would try to live up to his or her public image.

For a job interview, you want to reinforce the interviewer's impression that you're the right person for the job. Ideally you want to dress just as if you already worked there, but a bit more conservatively. You might try to be selective about style (tailored clothes look 'businesslike') and colour (warm tones make people respond 'warmly' towards the wearer). Find out where you can get advice and further information about such factors. Again, sort it out well in advance. Make sure it's clean, it's pressed, it fits. And – most important – make sure you're happy with how you look and feel.

As an exercise, check through your current wardrobe to find interview outfits that would be suitable for the sort of job you're interested in – one each for summer and winter.

Think about what other factors you might be able to plan for in advance.

Step 2

Build up your confidence. The most important thing to remember is that they're already interested in you, and that they probably already think you're capable of doing the job – otherwise you wouldn't have been asked. The main purpose of the interview is to get to know you. So be yourself – it's always easier than pretending to be someone you're not. In any case, if you were to get a job you're not right for, it's not likely to be right for you. Remember also that you want to get to know *them*.

Step 3

Relax. There are countless techniques and philosophies around that will help you to relax. Here is one that may work for you.

First, regularise your breathing. Breathe in deeply whilst counting slowly to six, hold it a moment, and then breath out again to the same slow count. Repeat several times.

Once you've built up a steady, deep rhythm, visualise yourself at the centre of a large spinning gyroscope. First, imagine a wide hoop spinning around your waist in a clockwise direction. When that is in place, add a second ring circling vertically around you, again in a clockwise direction, from above your head to under your feet and back up the other side. Finally, visualise a third hoop circling from front to back over your head and under your feet.

This visualisation can work in much the same way that a gyroscope keeps an aircraft or submarine steady – it stabilises the nerves in the midst of rolling chaos.

Exercise 2: They're not OK

Step 1

Relax. If the interviewers know what they're doing, they'll help you to relax. It's the chat show host's job to make the guest look good. It's also a personnel officer's job to put you at your ease, ask the right questions, and really get to know you. On the other hand, what if they don't?

Step 2

Consider the possibility that the interviewers may *not* always know what they're doing. If you're not comfortable – and if you're confident that you've done your homework – the chances are it's the interviewers' problem. They may be inexperienced. They may be more nervous than you are. The room may be arranged awkwardly.

What would you do in the following situations:

- *The Tennis Match*. The interviewers are placed either side of you, and you have to bounce your eye contact back and forth, from one to the other, just like Wimbledon. (Which one do you look at? Who's the boss?)
- *The Star Chamber*. You're at one end of a long table, facing a panel of interviewers at the other end of the room. There seems to be a mysterious protocol about what order they speak in, and it's going to be impossible to remember all their names and positions.
- *The Quiz Show*. The interviewer has a fixed set of questions, which he asks in precise order, taking notes as you answer. He hardly looks at you. You'll never know what the correct answers were.
- *The Bake-Off*. You and all the other short-listed candidates are herded into the same room and the interviews are conducted in front of everybody.

They may ask all the wrong questions (see Exercise 3). They may keep you waiting, mix up the paperwork, forget your name or do any number of things which indicate that their act isn't together.

What can you do about any of it? Smile. (In other words, grin and bear it.) Answer the questions as asked. Be understanding, helpful and informative. If you get the job, maybe you can sort them out before they inflict all that on another poor soul. On the other hand, you might consider carefully whether you really want to work for this company.

131

Exercise 3: Question time

Step 1

Try to anticipate what they might ask you. Remember that this is an exercise in selling, consider the features and benefits, and plan your answers to the following questions:

- Are you married? What does your husband do?
- Where do you live? How long have you lived there?
- How would you get to work? How long does it take?
- Can you drive? Do you have your own car? What sort?
- Do you have any children? How many, how old, girl(s) or boy(s)? If your children are young, they're likely to ask about your childcare arrangements.
- They might ask specific questions about your CV and your previous experience.
- Do you have any hobbies? What do you do to relax?
- If you're young they'll ask about school and exams.
- Why do you want this job?
- Do you know anything about the company?
- What are your ambitions?
- When could you start?
- Tell us a bit about yourself.

Don't be put off by the fact that many of these questions have nothing at all to do with the job or your ability to do it. Again, just answer the questions. Cheerfully. Seriously. Tell them what they want to know. Don't question the questioner's motive in asking them. It might just be an attempt to put you at your ease, or for the interviewer to get to know the *real* you. Try to turn the questions to your advantage (sell the benefits).

Step 2

'Tell us about yourself' is a well-established conversation stopper. Journalists learn quickly not to ask questions like that – they're guaranteed to create awkward silences in an interview. But interviewers are not always experienced enough to know this, so you have to be prepared.

Actors face this sort of thing daily. They wait for hours to be seen, finally get their turn, and the first thing the casting assistant might say is something like 'Tell us the story of your life in 30 seconds'. (It must be said, however, that the casting assistant may have talked to 200 actors in the last three hours.) The actors' response is to smile winningly and say something clever, or they won't get the part. At a job interview, you're in roughly the same position. What would you say?

Step 3

The final question in an interview is almost always 'Do *you* have any questions?' Here are a few that you might ask them (if they haven't already been covered):

- What is the history of the company? What else do they do? How many people do they employ?
- What are the working hours? Benefits? Holidays? Will you be paid weekly, fortnightly or monthly?
- When will you be told the result of the interview?
- When would they want you to start?

Can you think of any others? You need to ask only two or three questions at most. Ideally you'll want to ask questions that arise during the interview, relate directly to the company or the job, and which will demonstrate what an alert, interested, intelligent and capable person you are. The last question listed can be a good one to end with – it strikes a positive, confident note, and often it allows you to gauge how good a chance you have.

Exercise 4: Dos And Don'ts

Step 1

We'll start with some things to avoid:

- Don't accept a drink. If you do, it might be too hot, you might spill it, there might not be a convenient place to put it during the interview.
- Don't accept a cigarette if you smoke. If you do, the ashtray might be out of reach or overflowing. The smoke might go into the interviewer's eyes. You might cough.
- Don't sit down before you're asked to do so.
- Don't interrupt the interviewer – wait until he or she has finished speaking before you start to speak.
- Don't slouch back in the chair. Don't lean too far forward or sit on the edge of the chair. Just sit comfortably.
- Don't answer 'yes' or 'no' to questions. The interviewer wants to find out what you think.
- Don't drink alcohol before an interview – not even a small glass of wine with lunch.
- Don't be late. If you realise you are going to be unavoidably delayed, telephone the company, explain *briefly*, apologise *briefly*, tell them when you expect to arrive, and offer them the option to re-schedule your appointment.

Step 2

Things to do:

- Do try to smile. A friendly face makes a better impression than a nervous frown.
- Do say 'hello' and shake hands with your interviewer when you enter the room (another reason not to have a drink in your hand). Say 'thank you' before you leave.
- Do try to show your interest in and enthusiasm for the work you're being interviewed for.
- Do believe that you have as much in your favour as anyone else – otherwise they wouldn't be talking to you.

Believe in your own ability to do the job, and you will be able to convince others that you are capable.

Exercise 5: Practice

There aren't a lot of ways to practise for interviews, except to do it. You might enlist a friend to role play an interview situation with you, so that you can rehearse some of your answers. Exchanging roles will also give you an idea of how difficult the situation can be for the interviewer – always a useful thing to remember.

If you're genuinely looking for a job, you might find it helpful to arrange an appointment at your local Careers Office. The advice session will be useful, and it might serve to prime you for a job interview. Job Centre personnel sometimes do a preliminary interview before referring candidates. And you might register with – and be interviewed by – any number of employment agencies. All three of these situations are comparable to a job interview and will help bolster your confidence, because they're less threatening – in each case the interviewer is likely to be 'on your side'.

Finally, hold this thought: the more interviews you do, the easier it should become.

17

Decision-making

You might say that freedom of choice is the ultimate aim of Equal
Opportunities legislation, the Women's Liberation movement,
and all the various self-help courses and books that are now
available to women. It means, in simple terms, being offered the
same opportunities and guaranteed the same rights as anyone to
choose what you want to do and then do it. Having the freedom
to choose implies that you are willing and able to make decisions,
and that you will take responsibility for the consequences of your
choice.

In this chapter we are going to lay to rest all the old cliches that
tell us that women are indecisive: 'Women don't know their own
minds'. 'Women can't make up their minds.' 'It's a woman's
prerogative to change her mind.' 'What do women want?'
'Women don't know what they want.' All of those can be
dismissed as bad old jokes – simplistic propaganda that only
serves to undermine our self-confidence. By way of illustration,
consider the following hypothetical case.

Mr and Mrs Q are shopping for a widget. They want to spend
no more than £10. Mrs Q visits all the widget shops in the High
Street, looks at all the different models, compares features and
prices, and asks Mr Q and the sales clerk what they think. She
considers the choices for a bit, and then goes back to the third
widget shop to buy the one she believes is best value. She
admits, however, that she's not entirely confident she's made
the right choice.

Meanwhile, Mr Q – having become impatient with his wife's 'indecisiveness' – walks into the first widget shop he sees and asks for a widget. Since it only costs £9.95, he buys the first one he is shown.

Which one do you think would be called 'decisive'? Which of them is likely to have made the better decision?

Exercise 1: Snap decisions

People naturally take actions throughout their lives, often without being aware that there are any alternatives, that they have a choice, or even that they've made a choice. Are they blundering ahead without thinking, or are they just doing the obvious, following the path of least resistance?

We often make snap decisions – sometimes because there's no time to weigh the pros and cons. These decisions rarely carry heavy consequences – usually it's something like choosing what to order in a restaurant (the waiter is standing over you, losing patience), or buying on impulse (a favourite in the retail trade). Sometimes, however, we're pressured into making a snap decision when it really deserves more thought.

Think of two recent occasions when you made a snap decision that didn't really work out well. For each of them, answer the following questions, making notes to help clarify your thinking:

- What did you make the decision about?
- Why did it have to be a snap decision?
- What did you want to happen?
- What actually happened?
- With hindsight, what would you change about your original decision to get the result you wanted?

Exercise 2: Types of decision

Broadly speaking, there are three sorts of circumstances when you have to make decisions: *no choice*, *restricted choice*, and *free choice*.

Step 1

List two examples of decisions you've made in *no choice*, *restricted choice*, and *free choice* situations.

- *No choice*. This is a situation where you have no choice as to whether you take a particular action. Often it is legally enforced. Examples are such things as paying tax or educating your children. You might be able to choose *how* you do it (for instance, you can teach your children at home, send them to a private school, or send them to the local authority school). But you have no choice on *whether* to do it, because education is mandatory for children up to age 16.
- *Restricted choice*. In this situation, you have some control over the choices open to you, but there are also some expectations from others. One common example is the set menu at your favourite Chinese take-away: you may be able to choose from amongst several dishes, but if the restrictions imposed are 'one from Column A and two from Column B', you're not likely to persuade them to substitute three from Column A.
- *Free choice*. In this case, there are no restrictions – either imposed by others or dictated by your circumstances – on the choice you make. If you have blue, black, brown, gray, red, green and purple socks, it's entirely up to you which colour you choose to wear. Assuming that no one has imposed a dress code, you might even choose a different colour sock for each foot.

You're unlikely to be given a totally free choice in most decisions, but usually there will be a range of options to choose from.

In many circumstances you'll make a decision almost without realising it. When you're driving a car, for instance, most of your choices will be instinctive. In other cases, you need to give a great deal of consideration to your choice, but you can't opt out of the responsibility for making a decision. If you choose to leave decision-making to others, you give away your right to criticise the result, however much you might disagree with it.

Step 2

The following are some examples of actions which any of us might take as the result of certain decisions.

- Getting up this morning.
- Paying your community charge.
- Paying VAT on shoes.
- Getting married.
- Not having to pay to see an NHS doctor.
- Reading this book.
- Moving house.
- Buying a newspaper.

Were each of these:

(a) a decision made without realising it?
(b) a decision needing careful deliberation?
(c) a decision made by others which you find unacceptable?
    or
(d) a decision made by others which you find acceptable?

Step 3

Think about other decisions you have made. List two for each of the four categories (a), (b), (c), and (d) above.

Exercise 3: Important decisions – past

It would take quite a stretch of imagination to demonstrate how your choice of particular dishes from a Chinese menu on a particular night could vitally affect the rest of your life. However, it will be a useful exercise to put into perspective at least some of the more significant decisions you've made in the course of a lifetime.

Step 1

Think about the serious decisions you've made in your life, starting from the age of ten. Make a list of at least ten of them. Number the list in chronological order, noting how old you were at the time you made the decision. Then rate each decision according to how important you considered it at the time: Vital, Very Important, Fairly Important, or Not Important. Then note how you feel about each decision now: was it more or less important than you'd expected it to be? In hindsight, should you have considered your options more carefully?

Example:
The following are some decisions in the life of a 42-year-old woman.

1. Examinations to be taken at secondary school. Didn't seem very important at the time, as I just wanted to leave school and get a job in a shop. Didn't think much about how this decision might affect me in the future.
2. Left school/first job. Wanted a job near home, didn't think about prospects or money.
3. Went to work abroad. Important, as I had to convince my parents and myself that this was okay.
4. Came back from abroad. Now I wish I had given this more thought, as I might have had a completely different life if I had decided to stay or go somewhere else.
5. Drifted through various jobs. No real thought or decisions made. Usually moved on when I felt like a change.

6. Got married. Very important decision, but not sure now how much thought really went into it.
7. Bought first house. Very important decision about how much we could afford, location and so forth.
8. Had first child. Should have been a vital decision, but not sure it wasn't just expected of me.
9. Likewise with second child.
10. No more children. Very definite decision, followed through with help of family planning clinic.

Step 2

Draw a chart like the one below, indicating Vital, Very Important, Fairly Important, Not Important – one line for each – in the left column. Across the bottom, indicate years of age, ten through to sixty-five. Draw a vertical line through the chart at your current age. Enter your decisions on the chart, at the appropriate age and level of importance at the time, as shown for our example.

```
Vital               ————————————8—9-10 | ——————————
Very important  ————————3——6-7———————  | ——————————
Fairly important ————————4 —————————    | ——————————
Not important   ——1–2————5 ——————————  | ——————————
  Your age      10  15  20  25  30  35  40  45  50  55  60  65
```

Step 3

If, in hindsight, you now believe that any of those decisions were more or less important than you thought they were at the time, use a different coloured pen to enter them again on the appropriate line.

What does the chart tell you about the way you've made major decisions in your life? Is there a pattern? Is there room for improvement in your decision-making process? You should now be more aware of how easy it is to 'let things happen to you' without consciously taking responsibility for making your own decisions.

Exercise 4: Consequences

Step 1

Consider the following: Your alarm clock is ringing. It is a cold, dark morning. The bed is warm and comfortable. You are supposed to get up and go to work, but you feel tired. You need to make a decision based on available options. What are your options?

Basically, you have two choices: you can get up or you can stay in bed. There is also, of course, the compromise option of staying in bed a little longer. What are the consequences of each option to yourself, and to others? You might fill in your answers on a grid like the following:

Options	Effects of decision made	
	On yourself	*On others*
Get up & go to work		
Stay in bed for a while		
Stay in bed, forget work		

Step 2

Repeat the exercise. All of the above circumstances still hold true, expect that now you are a heart transplant surgeon. On your operating list for today are a number of patients whose lives may be in danger if you don't operate.

Obviously, if you are a surgeon, the consequences of staying in bed all day can be very different from the consequences if you are an accounts clerk or a ballet dancer. Your actions will be motivated by a different set of priorities. Whether the motivation is saving lives, feeding your family, or 'the show must go on' – everyone's motivation is valid, everyone has to set appropriate goals, and everyone has to take the consequences for whatever line of action is chosen.

The decision tree

Decision-making is a straightforward and logical process of working through the options. Chess players do it in their heads. Graduate business students do it on paper. The method they're taught is called a Decision Tree. Anyone can do it. It's a 5-step process:

1. Identify all the possible options that you have.
2. List the pros and cons for each option.
3. Sort the options according to whether they have more pros or cons.
4. Think through the likely consequences for each possible course of action ('What happens if . . . ?').
5. Choose the action that appears to give the best result, implement it, and compare what actually happens against your expected result.

In diagram form, a decision tree might look like this:

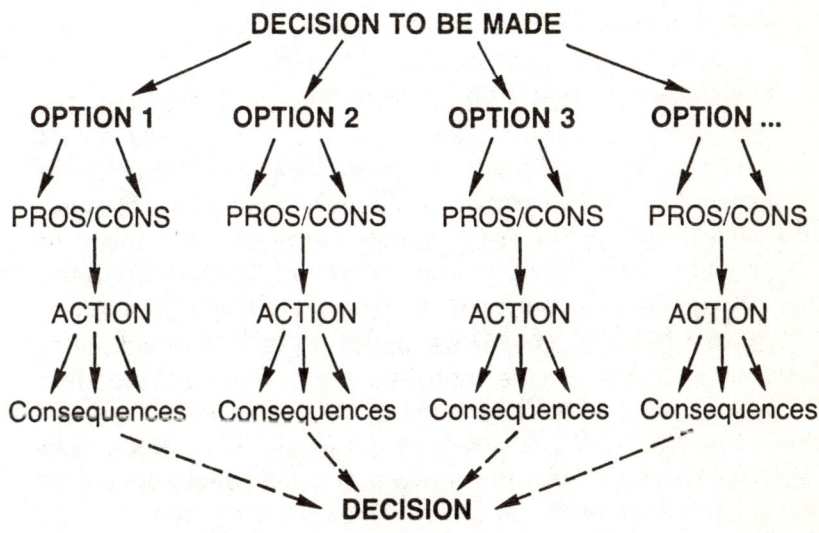

Exercise 5: The decision tree

Imagine you are going to buy a second-hand car. The only apparent restriction is financial – you can spend up to £2,000. Try using a Decision Tree to work out the best course of action:

- List as many of your options as you can think of. You might consider: whether to buy from a dealer you know and trust, from a dealer you know nothing about, from a newspaper ad, from a friend, or from an auction; whether to buy a fairly new car or to buy an old car and run it into the ground; choices between foreign or British-made cars, estate or saloon, colours, and a range of other features.
- What are the pros and cons of each of the options? If you buy from a dealer, for instance, you may get a guarantee, but the car will probably cost more than if you buy at auction. Write the pros and cons down under each option.
- Based on a comparison of the pros and cons, which are the three most promising lines of action?
- What are the consequences – good and bad – that are likely to result from each line of action? List them.
- After weighing the consequences and possible knock-on effects, what compromises are you prepared to make?
- What appears to be the best action? And why?

It's quite possible that the decision you end up making will not be what you intended at the outset. Sometimes that is the result of how much you know. A Trading Standards officer might know more about the reliability of dealers than a mechanic. A mechanic would probably know more about the reliability of the engine or the gearbox. You might not know as much as you would like about either.

There is always an element of risk in decision-making. You can cut down the risk factor by finding out as much information as you can about each of your options. You can compromise – buy a blue car when you'd really prefer red. You can also try to anticipate the knock-on effects of your choice. But at some point you have to accept the risk and go for a particular course of action.

Exercise 6: Important decisions – future

We're now going to apply some of the theory we've worked on so far in this chapter to your own real-life decisions.

Step 1

Think about some of the decisions you are likely to need to make in the future. Make a chart like the one below, ruling five columns. Down the left-hand side, list Not Important, Fairly Important, Very Important, and Vital – one per line. The other four columns will indicate a timescale for the decisions you're facing: In the next week, in the next month, in the next year, and in the next five years.

	Decisions to be made			
	In the next week	In the next month	In the next year	In the next 5 years
Not important				
Fairly important				
Very important				
Vital				

Write the decisions you want to consider into the appropriate spaces. Try to fill every block on the grid.

Step 2

Choose either the decision that you feel is Very Important and has to be made in the next month, or the decision that is Vital and has to be made in the next year. Work through the Decision Tree, by writing your answers to the following questions:

- What decision has to be made?
- List the options (as many as you think are relevant), with the pros and cons of each.
- What are the three most promising lines of action? What consequences – good and bad – can you see as a result of each?
- What compromises are you prepared to make, based on the possible consequences and knock-on effects?
- Which of these appears to be the best action? Why?

At this point you may find it useful to talk through your decision with a trusted friend or adviser. They may see the situation from a different perspective, which may inspire you with new ideas and fresh solutions. Remember, however, no matter how much advice you get, or who you use as a sounding board – *it's your choice*.

We'll have a look at some of your options in the next chapter

18

Options

What do you do now? Answer a question with a question: go back to the beginning and ask yourself what you wanted out of this book. Why did you start it in the first place? What was it meant to accomplish for you?

Most women who sign up for any kind of self-improvement course – or who read a self-help book like this one – probably start with a range of expectations. More importantly, they're likely to have taken it on in the first place, because they have expectations of themselves which they think they're not living up to. They're not happy as they are. They believe they should be – or should be doing – something more, something different, something better.

By the end of the course, their expectations are likely to have changed. Their goals probably have shifted. Their 'positive outcomes' – and there is almost always a positive outcome – may not be at all what they expected.

You may have reached the conclusion that You're OK just as you are. You're already doing what you do best, and on reflection it makes you happy. That is certainly a positive outcome.

You may have a good idea of what you would like to do next, but aren't ready to do it just yet – perhaps the time or the circumstances still aren't right. Well, fine. You know yourself better, and you should have developed a bit more confidence in your own abilities. You may have been able to pinpoint where any obstacles might be, and you've been working on the skills needed to do something about them. That is a positive outcome.

You may have identified one or more changes you'd like to make in your personal life, your relationships or the way you communicate with the people around you. You've had the opportunity to make a start on implementing those changes, and you're well able to continue making progress. That is a positive outcome.

You may have discovered some subjects that you'd like to learn more about. Exploring them will be a positive action.

You may have decided to go back to work, change jobs, start your own business – or you may have recognised that there are things you need to learn before you can do any of those.

In this chapter we're going to look briefly at some of these options: specifically, options available to you in employment, self-employment and further training.

Exercise 1: Employment

Step 1

What do you want to do? If you haven't already arrived at a firm decision, refer back to your work on Skills and Aptitudes. The Skills Stocktake you completed in Chapter 6, in particular, will help you begin to explore possible areas of work that appeal to you, and which you're suited for. Completing the following checklist should also help clarify your thoughts. Tick as appropriate:

	YES	NO	DON'T MIND
I would be prepared to:			
Work out of doors			
Use my hands			
Keep clean when working			
Handle paperwork			
Follow instructions			
Be smartly dressed			
Work unsocial hours			
Work under pressure			
Work with the public			
Concentrate for long periods			

contd.	*YES*	*NO*	*DON'T MIND*
Work on my own initiative			
Travel to work			
Work in difficult conditions			
Care for others			
Do repetitive work			
Take responsibility			
Work with numbers			
Get up early			
Work regular hours			
Work sitting down			
Carry out a variety of tasks			
Keep learning new things			
Do fine or accurate work			
Work in a team or a group			

At the end of the above list, add at least three other conditions or aspects of work which are important to you. (For instance, if you are prone to allergies, that would be an important consideration in your working environment.)

You might want to talk these through with a friend. If you need further advice, your local Job Centre, Careers Office or Community Education Office may be able to offer guidance or possibly aptitude testing.

Step 2

When you've arrived at a particular job, or an area to explore, do a bit of research about which skills are realistically needed, and what the job is really like. Start with a 'common sense' analysis, and then check against job adverts and descriptions or, again, seek advice at the Careers Office, Employment Agencies, Job Centres and so forth. The best possible research would be to try and contact someone who's actually doing this sort of job. Try to find out as much information as you can:

• What opportunities are there in your area for this sort of job?

- What skills or qualifications are required for the job?
- What are the normal paths to follow to get this sort of job? Find out from people doing the job, how they were able to get it.
- Find out about salary, prospects and working conditions.
- Make a list of definite and possible vacancies, with addresses and phone numbers.

Step 3

Chart the skills that you've determined are necessary for the job or profession you're interested in. After each skill listed, indicate whether you already know how to do it, whether you need to improve your skills, or whether you'd need to learn it:

SKILL NEEDED	I CAN ALREADY DO THIS	I NEED TO IMPROVE	I WILL NEED TRAINING
(*list skills here*)			

Step 4

If, on balance, the indicators are 'yes' – and especially if you've learned about a definite vacancy – go for it! Edit your CV accordingly, write a good covering letter, and then check your wardrobe for something appropriate to wear to the interview.

If, on the other hand, you want to explore further possibilities, go on to Exercise 2.

Exercise 2: Self-employment

Step 1

What are the differences between being an employee and being self-employed? On balance it's a choice between security and defined responsibilities on the one hand versus flexibility and satisfaction on the other. Completing the chart below will help you to explore whether or not self-employment is what you really want:

	SELF-EMPLOYED	EMPLOYEE
Getting work	You have to find work to keep busy	Your boss finds the work
Doing work		
Getting paid		
How much pay?		
Sick leave		
Hours worked		
Pension		
Tax		
Satisfaction		
Responsibility		

Add any other factors you can think of where there might be a difference that would be relevant to you.

Step 2

The two best reasons to become self-employed are:

- you're already working in the field, and you believe you could do better on you own than you are working for an employer; or
- you have a brilliant idea. Many women, however, choose self-employment simply because it is convenient – it can allow them the flexibility to meet family commitments whilst earning a living. They may decide to go self-employed before they even have an idea.

Here are twenty ways to come up with an idea – try to think of an existing example for each, and then see if you can come up with something new:

1. copying somebody else's successful idea
2. combining two or more ideas in a new way
3. solving problems for people
4. finding out what the 'competition' is bad at
5. developing your hobby
6. building on your skills
7. turning waste materials into something useful
8. bringing ideas home from your holiday
9. brainstorming in a group
10. talking and listening to people
11. making lists and playing around with them
12. looking for gaps in the market
13. finding new ways to do things
14. improving a product or service
15. daydreaming and fantasising
16. doing market research
17. looking at what things *do* rather than what they *are*
18. listening when people say 'If only . . .'
19. always being on the lookout for opportunities
20. thinking in new ways: sideways, backwards, big, small.

Step 3

Success in business can be summed up in fairly simple terms: 'The right product to the right customer at the right time and at the right price.' Some of the factors going into that principle – no matter what sort of business you might consider going into – are a common core of basic business skills which can be learned. What is harder to pinpoint are the hidden factors and personal insight needed to make a business successful. Add to the following lists of skills needed for business success:

Standard business skills
Marketing
Publicity
Advertising
Financial records

Personal qualities
Sense of timing
Fulfilling deadlines
Attention to detail
Good communication

There are numerous sources of guidance available to people interested in setting up their own business. If you want to pursue this line, you can seek advice from banks, enterprise agencies, the Small Firms Service, colleges, and training organisations. There are any number of good publications and courses on offer, many of them free.

Exercise 3: Training

Whether you're interested in employment, self-employment, or some option as yet undetermined, it's entirely possible that you will benefit from training. The following should help you decide whether, what and where.

Step 1

Locate the following sources of information on training nearest you. For each of them, list the name, address, telephone number, and the name of a person to talk to about careers/employment/self-employment/training:

local library; careers office; college(s); school(s); other training organisations; enterprise agencies; Job Centre; sources of grants: what, where, how much, and how to apply; and any other relevant information.

Step 2

Select either the job possibility you explored in Exercise 1, or a self-employment idea which interested you in Exercise 2. Using the Yellow Pages, the library, brochures from local colleges and training organisations, and any other sources of information you have discovered, answer the following:

- What is the career/business you've chosen to investigate?
- What skills are needed in the job?
- What skills would you need more training in? (Refer to the checklist in Exercise 1 Step 3 . Repeat it if necessary.)
- List as many organisations as you can find which can help with training in your subject.
- What qualifications do you need to obtain?
- Are there any grants available, and where from? How much? How do you apply?
- Find at least three people locally who have the same career, and find out about their training, their career path, and where they get their advice.
- Record all the contacts you make, including names, addresses and telephone numbers.

Exercise 4: Decisions

Work through a Decision Tree on the options you've explored in this chapter. Weigh them against any other choices you're considering. Narrow your options to the best course of action, and then see Chapter 19.

19

Action planning – 3

You already know how to do everything in this chapter. The exercises use skills you developed earlier in the process. This time, however, it's not just for practice – it's for real.

Exercise 1: Goal setting (six months)

Step 1

List your goals for the next six months. Write them down, as quickly as possible, including:

- things you want to achieve;
- things you want to do; and
- things you want to happen.

Go for quantity, not quality. List goals quickly, as they come to mind. Don't try to put them in order of priority or timescale. Put down *everything* that comes to mind, no matter how incredible, ridiculous or trivial it might appear. You'll get a chance to sort them out later. *Do not censor yourself!*

Step 2

Sort the list by timescale. Depending on when in the next six months you want to achieve each of these goals, categorise them as follows: M1 – within the next month; M2 – within two months; and so forth to M6.

Step 3

Mark your goals 'A', 'B', or 'C' according to their importance ('A' most important, 'C' least). Work quickly, don't agonise – trust your instincts!

Step 4

Rank your goals in order of priority. First, cross out all the Bs and Cs, regrading any if necessary. Next rank the As in order of priority, starting with A1 as most important, A2 next, and so forth.

Exercise 2: Six-month action plan

Having set your goals, you'll now want to put them into action.

Step 1

Sort your A goals according to timescale, grouping M1s together, M2s, M3s and so forth. For each set of goals, fill in a chart like the following:

GOALS: (*list your M1 goals*)

What has to be done	Priority A,B,C,D	Start when	Finish by	Who by	Resources needed	Completed

---

Think carefully about what needs to be done to accomplish these goals, and list them in terms of positive actions. Keep your planned actions close to you in terms of responsibility, so that you're more likely to be able to influence the outcome. Talk through the process with a friend to help clarify your thinking.

Following the chart, list each task separately under 'what has to be done' and fill in the other columns as you go. (The 'completed' column will be ticked later when you accomplish the task.) For each action:

- decide on a specific timescale
- work out what resources you will need
- allocate responsibility for carrying out each action
- keep it realistic
- think about what support you will need.

Work carefully, think through each action completely, anticipating as many factors as possible.

Step 2

When you have listed every action you can think of, prioritise them using the system we used in Chapter 3: tasks which are Urgent and Important are Priority A, Urgent and Not Important are Priority B, Not Urgent but Important are Priority C, and Not Urgent and Not Important are Priority D.

Step 3

Repeat the entire process for your M2, M3, M4, M5 and M6 lists. If any of the tasks for later goals need to be started earlier, enter them under the appropriate month, with a notation (perhaps in a different colour pen) on which goals they're in aid of.

Step 4

Use the monthly action plans to gauge your progress in achieving your goals. Fill in the final column ('completed') as each task is accomplished. If you seem to be getting behind, don't let it get you down: simply re-allocate your time and priorities to allow yourself to catch up.

Step 5

It's not at all unlikely that your priorities – and your goals – may change over the next six months. Review occasionally, and make whatever adjustments in your action plan are necessary.

Conclusion

There isn't really a concluding chapter to this book. In the course of reading it, you have looked at various aspects of your life from a new perspective. You have learned and practised a number of techniques to help you determine what you want to do and then achieve it. A concluding chapter would, of course, have to be different for everybody.

Exercise 1: Conclusion

Write a concluding chapter to this book. Look back through the entire sequence of exercises to get an overview of what you, personally, have accomplished and how far you have come. Has the process lived up to your expectations so far? What did you enjoy most? What did you find most difficult? Have you accomplished what you set out to do? Have your expectations and goals changed? What would you have done differently? (The beauty of that last question is that there's nothing to stop you from doing it again, differently.)

List your positive outcomes. Which sets of 'muscles' have the exercises helped you to develop? Which do you still need or want to work on? What are the implications for the future and where might you go from here?

159

Exercise 2: The sequel

What you've done so far has been the beginning of an ongoing process of growth and development, which – if you so choose – may continue for the rest of your life. What you do next (the 'sequel') is entirely up to you.

In the last few chapters, we explored a few of the options open to you, and suggested where you might go for information and assistance. At the back of the book, you'll find a selection of books for a more in-depth look at some of the subjects and techniques we've worked on. We've also included a fairly substantial list of Useful Contacts – organisations, advice lines, agencies – which might help you as you continue to pursue the goals you set for yourself and carry out your Action Plan.

Exercise 3: Well done!

Give yourself high marks for persistence, honesty, understanding and courage. (You may add to this list as you see fit.)

Further reading

Alston, Anna and Miller, Ruth, *Hours to Suit*, Rosters, 1989

Barker, Dennis, *Fresh Start*, Rosters, 1990

Berne, Eric, *Games People Play*, Penguin, 1983

British Telecom, *Yellow Pages*

Burr, Rosemary, and Harris, Jenny, *Financial Choice for Women*, Rosters, 1990

Cameron, Janet, *The Competitive Woman*, Mercury Books, 1990

Chapman, Jane, *Women Working It Out*, COIC

Davidson, Marilyn and Cooper, Cary, *Working Women: An International Survey*, John Wiley & Sons, 1984

Davies, Philippa, *Your Total Image*, Piatkus Books, 1990

Dickson, Anne, *A Woman in Your Own Right*, Quartet Books, 1982

Fowler, Deborah, *The Woman's Guide to Starting Your Own Business*, Thorsons Publishing, 1988

Garratt, Sally, *Manage Your Time*, Fontana Paperbacks, 1985

Gray, Marianne, *The Freelance Alternative*, Piatkus Books, 1987

Grewal, Harjit, *The Sex Discrimination Handbook*, Sphere Books, 1990

Harris, Jean, *Everything You Need to Know for Success in Business – The Woman's Guide*, Thorsons Publishing, 1990

Harris, Thomas, *I'm OK, You're OK*, Pan Books, 1973

Hawkins, Barrie, and Bage, Grant, *Think Up A Business*, Rosters, 1990

HMSO, *Health and Safety at Work*

161

Hopson, Dr Barrie and Scally, Mike, *Build Your Own Rainbow – A Workbook for Career and Life Management*, Mercury Books, 1990

Hopson, Dr Barrie, Scally, Mike and Stafford, Kevern, *Transitions – The Challenge of Change*, Mercury Books, 1992

Johnson, Ron, *The 24 Hour Business Plan*, Hutchinson Business Books, 1990

Korving, Margaret, *Training for Your Next Career*, Rosters, 1989

Manning, Marilyn and Haddock, Patricia, *Leadership Skills for Women*, Kogan Page, 1989

McBennett, Ross, *Starting Up Your Own Business – 101 Ways To Do It on £5000 or Less*, Mercury Business Paperbacks, 1990

O'Connor, Joyce and Ruddle, Helen, *Business Matters for Women*, Attic Press, 1990

O'Connor, Joyce and Ruddle, Helen, *You Can Do It – A Life and Work Skills Book for Women*, Gill & MacMillan, 1989

Palmer, Penny et al., *WMA Returners Pack*, Working Mothers Association, 1990

Parkes, Colin Murray, *Bereavement: Studies of Grief in Adult Life*, Penguin, 1986

Scott, Ian (transl. & ed.), *The Lüscher Colour Test*, Pan Books, 1987

Sheehy, Gail, *Passages: Predictable Crises of Adult Life*, Dutton, 1976

Shepard, Dr Martin, *Do-It-Yourself Psychotherapy*, Macdonald Optima, 1988

Tysoe, Dr Maryon, *All This and Work Too – The Psychology of Office Life*, Fontana Paperbacks, 1988

Watkins, David et al., *Be Your Own Boss – Starter Kit*, National Extension College, 1986

Which? Books, *Earning Money At Home – How to Brush Up A Skill or Hobby to Money-making Standards*, Consumers' Association, Hodder & Stoughton, 1989

Willis, Liz and Daisley, Jenny, *Springboard – Women's Development Workbook*, Kogan Page, 1990

Useful contacts

Academic Women's Achievement Group
University College London
Gower Street
London WC1E 6BT
Tel: (071) 387-7050 & (071) 380-7232

ACAS Head Office
11/12 St James's Square
London SW1Y 4LA
Tel: (071) 210-3000

Action Resource Centre (ARC)
1st Floor
102 Park Village East
London NW1 3SP
Tel: (071) 383-2200

The Adult Training Promotions Unit
Room 212
Department of Education and Science
Elizabeth House
York Road
London SE1 7PH
Tel: (071) 934-0859

Advisory Conciliation & Arbitration Service (ACAS)
Clifton House
83-118 Euston Road
London NE1 2RB
Tel (071) 388-5100

The Arts Council
105 Piccadilly
London W1V 0AU
Tel: (071) 333-0100

Association of Women Solicitors
The Law Society
8 Bream's Buildings
London EC4A 1HP
Tel: (071) 404-4355

British Association of Women Entrepreneurs
303 Preston Road
Harrow
Middlesex HA3 0QQ
Tel: (081) 904-1412

British Institute of Management (BIM)
Small Firms Information Service
Management House
Cottingham Road
Corby
Northants NN17 1TT
Tel: (0536) 204222

Business in the Community
227A City Road
London EC1V 1LX
Tel: (071) 253-3716

Business Library
General Reference Dept
The Mitchell Laboratory
North Street
Glasgow G3 7DN
Tel: (041) 221-7030

Business Woman's Travel Club Ltd
520 Fulham Road
London SW6
Tel: (071) 384-1121

Career Development for Women
97 Mallard Place
Twickenham
Middlesex TW1 4SW
Tel: (081) 892-3806

Central Office of Information
Hercules Road
London SE1 7DU
Tel: (071) 928-2345

The Centre for European Business Information
Small Firms Service
Ebury Bridge House
2-18 Ebury Bridge Road
London SW1W 8QD
Tel: (071) 828-6201

Centre for Research On European Women
38 Rue Stevin
1040 Brussels
Belgium
Tel: (010322) 2309479

COIC (Career & Occupational Information Centre)
Moorfoot
Sheffield S1 4PQ
Tel: (0742) 753275 or 594859

Commission of the European Communities
Jean Monet House
8 Storeys Gate
London SW1P 3AT
Tel: (071) 222-8122

Commission for Racial Equality
Elliot House
10/12 Allington Street
London SW1E 5EH
Tel: (071) 828-7022

Commonwealth & Secretariat – Women & Development
Programme
Marlborough House
Pall Mall
London SW1Y 5HX
Tel: (071) 839-3411

Co-operative Development Agency
Unit 15, The Arches Industrial Estate
Spond End
Coventry CV1 3JQ
Tel: (0203) 714078

The Council for the Accreditation
of Correspondence Colleges (CACC)
27 Marylebone Road
London NW1 5JS
Tel: (071) 935-5391

The Crafts Council/The Crafts Advisory Committee
1 Oxendon Street
London SW1Y 4AT
Tel: (071) 930-4811

The Department of Employment
(Administrative Headquarters)
Caxton House
Tothill Street
London SW1H 9NF
Tel: (071) 273-3000

The Department of Employment
(Wages Inspectorate)
Clifton House
2nd Floor
83/117 Euston Road
London NW1 2RB
Tel: (071) 387-2511

Department of Social Security (DSS)
Hannibal House
Newington Causeway
Elephant & Castle
London SE1 6BY
Tel: (071) 972-2000

Design Council
28 Haymarket
London SW1Y 4SU
Tel: (071) 839-8000

Development Board for Rural Wales
Ladywell House
Newton
Powys SY16 1JB
Tel: (0686) 626965

Durham University Business School
Small Business Centre
Mill Hill Lane
Durham DH1 3LB
Tel: (091) 374-2211

Educational Media International
235 Imperial Drive
Rayners Lane
Harrow
Middlesex
Tel: (081) 868-1908 and (081) 868-1915

Useful contacts

English Tourist Board
Thames Tower
Blacks Road
Hammersmith
London W6 9EL
Tel: (081) 846-9000

Equal Opportunities Commission
Information Centre
Overseas House
Quay Street
Manchester M3 3HN
Tel: (061) 833-9244

EuroPACE Northern UK Centre
(European Programme of Advanced
Continuing Education)
Manchester Polytechnic
John Dalton Building
Chester Street
Manchester M1 5GD
Tel: (061) 247-1629

European Union of Women
32 Smith Square
Westminster
London SW1P 3HH
Tel: (071) 222-9000

European Women's Management Development Network (UK)
Ashbridge Management College
Berkhamsted
Herts HP4 1NS
Tel: (044) 284-3491

Every Woman Ltd
Freepost
London N1 8BR
Tel: (071) 633-3616

Federation of Business & Professional Women
23 Ansdell Street
London W8 5BN
Tel: (071) 938-1729

Focus Information Service
47/49 Gower Street
London WC1E 6HR
Tel: (071) 221-9600

Freefone Enterprise
Tel: 100
(Ask the Operator to connect you to your Freefone Enterprise Centre who will
have information on business problems and sources of help.)

Further Education Unit
Grove House
2 Orange Street
London WC2H 7WE
Tel: (071) 321-0433

Government Services
Department of the Environment
Five Ways Tower
Frederick Road
Edgbaston
Birmingham B15 1YT
Tel: (021) 626-2000

Government Services
Yorkshire & Humberside Regional Office
Department of the Environment
City House
New Station Street
Leeds LS1 4DJ
Tel: (0532) 438232

Government Services
Northern Regional Office
Department of the Environment
Wellbar House
Gallowgate
Newcastle upon Tyne NE1 4TD
Tel: (091) 232-7575

Government Services
Greater London Planning
Department of the Environment
Room C8/06
2 Marsham Street
London SW1P 3EB
Tel: (071) 217-4464

Government Services
North West Enterprise Unit
Department of the Environment
Sunley Building
Piccadilly Plaza
Manchester M1 4BE
Tel: (061) 832-9111

Government Services
South-East Regional Office
Department of the Environment
Charles House
375 Kensington High Street
London W14 8QH
Tel: (071) 605-9016

Government Services
Industry Department for Scotland
New St Andrew's House
St James Centre
Edinburgh EH1 3TB
Tel: (031) 556-8400

Government Services
Welsh Office
Cathays Park
Cardiff CF1 3NQ
Tel: (0222) 825111

Her Majesty's Stationery Office (HMSO)
Orders & Enquiries
P O Box 276
London SW8
Tel: (071) 873-0022

Her Majesty's Stationery Office
Retail Counter Service
Holborn Bookshop
49 High Holborn
London WC1
Tel: (071) 873-0011

Infolink PLC
Coombe Cross
2-4 South End
Croydon CR0 1DL
Tel: (081) 686-7777

Institute of Training & Development
Marlow House
Institute Road
Marlow
Buckinghamshire SL7 1BN
Tel: (0628) 890123

Kids' Clubs Network
279-281 Whitechapel Road
London E1 1BY
Tel: (071) 247-3009

The Lady
39-40 Bedford Street
London WC2E 9ER
Tel: (071) 379-4717

Learning from Experience Trust
Suite 210
Southbank House
Black Prince Road
London SE1 7SJ
Tel: (071) 587-0944

Leicester Outwork Campaign
116 St Peter's Road
Leicester LE2 1DE
Tel: (0533) 470940

Maternity Alliance
15 Britannia Street
London WC1X 9JP
Tel: (071) 837-1265

Medical Women's Federation
Tavistock House North
Tavistock Square
London WC1H 9HX
Tel: (071) 387-7765

National Association of Women Pharmacists
Pharmaceutical Society of Great Britain
1 Lambeth High Street
London SE1 7JN
Tel: (071) 582-1633

National Childminders Association (NCMA)
8 Mason's Hill
Bromley
Kent BR2 9EY
Tel: (081) 464-6164

National Council for Civil Liberties
21 Tabard Street
London SE1 4LA
Tel: (071) 403-3888

National Council of Women
36 Danbury Street
Islington
London N1 8JN
Tel: (071) 354-2395

National Federation of Beauty Therapists
PO Box 36
Arundel
West Sussex BN18 0SW
Tel: (0903) 883027

National Federation of Self-Employed & Small Businesses Ltd
32 St Anne's Road West
Lytham St Annes
Lancashire FY8 1NY
Tel: (0253) 720911

National Federation of Self-Employed & Small Businesses Ltd
The Press & Parliamentary Office
140 Lower Marsh
Westminster Bridge
London SE1 7AE
Tel: (071) 928-9272

National Federation of Spiritual Healers
Old Manor Farm Studio
Church Street
Sunbury-on-Thames
Middlesex TW16 6RG
Tel: (0932) 783164/5

National Homeworking Unit
3rd Floor
Wolverley House
18 Digbeth Street
Birmingham B5 6BJ
Tel: (021) 643-6352

National Institute for Adult & Continuing Education (NIACE)
19b De Montfort Street
Leicester LE1 7GE
Tel: (0533) 551451

National Institute for Adult & Continuing Education (NIACE)
WJEC Education Dept
245 Western Avenue
Cardiff CF5 2YX
Tel: (0222) 571201

National Organisation for Women's Management Education
12a Westbere Road
London NW2 3RR
Tel: (071) 794-8734

New Ways to Work
309 Upper Street
London N1 2TY
Tel: (071) 226-4026

New Working Woman
3 St Peters Buildings
York Street
Leeds LS9 8AJ
Tel: (0532) 432474

Nursery World Ltd
24-25 Cowcross Street
London EC1M 6DQ
Tel: (071) 837-7224

Office & Wages Councils
Steele House
11 Tothill Street
London SW1H 9NF
Tel: (071) 273-4812

The Open University
Walton Hall
Milton Keynes MK7 6AA
Tel: (0908) 274066

The Pre-School Playgroups Association
61 Kings Cross Road
London WC1
Tel: (071) 833-0991

Prince's Youth Business Trust
5 Cleveland Place
London SW1Y 6JJ
Tel: (071) 925-2900 & (071) 321-6500

Replan (Eastern Office)
Phoenix Chambers
15/17 High Street
Bedford MK40 1RN
Tel: (0234) 219832

Rights of Women (ROW)
52-54 Featherstone Street
London EC1Y 8RT
Tel: (071) 251-6577

Rights of Women Europe Group
10 Tredegar Road
London E3
Tel: (081) 980-4308

Rural Development Commission
141 Castle Street
Salisbury SP1 3TP
Tel: (0722) 336255

Scottish Enterprise Foundation
University of Stirling
Scotland FK9 4LA
Tel: (0786) 73171

Small Business Bureau
Suite 46
Westminster Palace Garden
Artillery Row
London SW1P 1RR
Tel: (071) 976-7262

Small Claims Court

(Booklets on Small Claims in the County Court
are available from any County Court.)

Small Firms Council
Centre Point
103 New Oxford Street
London WC1A 1DU
Tel: (071) 379-7400

The Small Firms Service
(now integrated into TECs)
Tel: (0742) 594776 to find your local centre.

Soroptimist International of Great Britain & Ireland
63 Bayswater Road
London W2 3PJ
Tel: (071) 723-1061

300 Group
9 Poland Street
London W1V 3DG
Tel: (071) 600-2390

Training Access Points (TAPS)
TAP Focus in Women Unit
College House
c/o 3 Ellison Place
Newcastle upon Tyne NE1 8ST
Tel: (091) 261-5357

Training & Enterprise Councils (TECs)
Department of Employment
Moorfoot
Sheffield S1 4PQ
Tel: (0742) 594776 for your local TEC number

Training Education & Enterprise Directorate (TEED)
Department of Employment
Room E405
Moorfoot
Sheffield S1 4PQ
Tel: (0742) 704667 or (0742) 753275

Vocational Guidance Association
7 Harley House
Upper Harley Street
London NW1 4RP
Tel: (071) 935-2600

Women Against Sexual Harassment (WASH)
242 Pentonville Road
London N1 9UN
Tel: (071) 833-0222

Women and Manual Trades
52-54 Featherstone Street
London EC1
Tel: (071) 251-9192/3

Women and Training Group
Hewmar House
120 London Road
Gloucester GL1 3TL
Tel: (0452) 309330

Women Architects Group
RIBA
66 Portland Place
London W1N 4AD
Tel: (071) 580-5533

Women in Banking
Target Life Assurance
Alton House
174/177 High Holborn
London WC1
Tel: (071) 629-1995

Women in Civil Service
Department of Industry
Ashdown House
123 Victoria Street
London SW1
Tel: (071) 275-5000

Women in Computing
c/o Micro Sister
Wesley House
4 Wild Court
London WC2
Tel: (071) 430-0655

Women in Enterprise
c/o Kay Smith Associates
St Gabriel's House
24 Laburnum Road
Wakefield WF1 3QS
Tel: (0924) 361876 for your regional branch

Women in Management
64 Marryat Road
Wimbledon
London SW19 5BN
Tel: (081) 944-6332

Women in Partnership
Commission of the European Communities
8 Storey's Gate
London SW1 3AT
Tel: (071) 222-8122

Women into Business
Small Business Bureau
32 Smith Square
London SW1P 3HH
Tel: (071) 976-7262

Women's Advertising Club of London
Donavon Data Systems
Berger House
7 Farm Street
London W1X 7RB
Tel: (071) 629-7654

Women's Computer Centre
Wesley House
4 Wild Court
London WC2B 5AX
Tel: (071) 430-0112

Women's Engineering Society
Imperial College of Science & Technology
Department of Civil Engineering
Imperial College Road
London SW7 2AZ
Tel: (071) 589-5111

Women's Enterprise Development Agency (WEDA)
Aston Science Park
Love Lane
Aston Triangle
Birmingham B7 4BJ
Tel: (021) 359-0981 and (021) 359-0178

Women's Film Television & Video Network
79 Wardour Street
London W1V 3PH
Tel: (071) 434-2076

Women's Independent Cinema House
c/o Merseyside Arts
Graphic House
Duke Street
Liverpool L1 4RJ
Tel: (051) 709-2439

Women's Motor Mechanics Workshop Ltd
Bay 4R
1-3 Brixton Road
London SW9 6DE
Tel: (071) 582-2574

Women's Travel Club of Great Britain
Atlantida Travel
21 Garrick Street
London WC2E 9AZ
Tel: (071) 240-2888

Worker's Education Association (WEA)
Temple House
9 Upper Berkeley Street
London W1H 8BY
Tel: (071) 402-5608

Working for Childcare/Workplace Nurseries
77 Holloway Road
London N7 8JZ
Tel: (071) 700-0281

Useful contacts

Working Mothers' Association
77 Holloway Road
London N7 8JZ
Tel: (071) 700-5771